連珠不断亭
立石樹木の
庭よろしく
で久する

本國寺中
和持院庭

Japanese Gardens

Günter Nitschke

Japanese Gardens

Right Angle and Natural Form

TASCHEN

KÖLN LONDON MADRID NEW YORK PARIS TOKYO

© 1999 Benedikt Taschen Verlag GmbH
Hohenzollernring 53, D–50672 Köln
Design: Detlev Schaper, Michael Ditter, Cologne
Cover: Angelika Taschen, Cologne
English translation: Karen Williams, London

Printed in Italy
ISBN 3–8228–7633–X

Contents

Introduction

This very place the Lotus Paradise,
this very body the Buddha.
Hakuin Zenshi: Song of Enlightenment

It has taken major ecological disasters to remind humankind that our earth is both a living and a conscious entity. Even the most hardened materialist must concede that stones, plants, animals and men are all inseparable elements of the natural whole. Rooted in our Western traditions, we find it hard to credit the Eastern belief that a rock has consciousness. Not because we know it is fallacious, but because we cannot measure it scientifically. Yet we are generally prepared to ascribe a degree of consciousness to plants and animals. We may even accept that, when a human being becomes conscious of himself as part of the earth, and of the earth as part of the universe, so the universe itself thereby becomes conscious of itself. Harder to understand, however, is the concept of a human being attaining enlightenment, i.e. of consciousness becoming aware of itself. At this delicate moment, so Eastern mystics believe, a flower opens in the "garden" of the universe. It is a moment of ultimate cosmic implosion, comparable only with that moment of original cosmic explosion we know as the Big Bang.

The enlightened mind finds the Lotus Paradise everywhere. For ordinary mortals, on the other hand, it is sought in gardens. The history of the Japanese garden is the history of man's search for his place within nature and thereby, ultimately, his search for himself. It is the aim of this book to document the most important historical stages in this search.

Although there remains much to be written on the Japanese garden in Western languages, Japan itself produces a wealth of scholarly literature on the subject.

Every month sees the publication of at least two or three new magazines and books devoted to the garden. The 36 volumes of "The Great Compendium of Japanese Garden History" by Mirei Shigemori and his son Kanto proved indispensable to my research. The majority of the sketches of Japanese gardens contained in this book are simplified versions of the drawings to which Shigemori devoted a lifetime's work. I consider it a great privilege to have met Shigemori several times before his death since I first embarked upon a book on the Japanese garden in 1967.

I also wish to thank the many others who have contributed so generously towards the project: Benito Boari for the drawings on pages 19–63, Jens Hvass for the drawings on pages 64–88, and Irina Detlefsen who supplied the majority of the remaining artwork. My warmest thanks also go to Ken Kawai from Kyoto University who performed a very large part of the Japanese correspondence and library research on my behalf. Irina Detlefsen and Ken Kawai also very kindly placed at my disposal a number of their own photographs, reflections of their own profound interest in the subject of the Japanese garden. I am also greatly indebted to Hiroshi Kojima, Director of the Imperial Household Agency in Kyoto, who made it possible for me to photograph the Katsura Palace garden at my leisure and who generously supplied some of the photographs of the Imperial Palace in Kyoto.
I thank Cid Corman for his gracious help in rendering some of the quoted Japanese poems into living English.

The Japanese sense of beauty:
The veneration of the unique in nature and the perfection of the man-made type

The Japanese garden is not simply nature, not simply "self-created", as the literal translation of the Japanese word for nature – *shizen* – would have us believe. The Japanese garden is and has always been nature crafted by man. It belongs to realm of architecture and is, at its best, nature as art.

In Japan, as in many other cultures, the garden traces its origins back to the first urban settlements and palaces. It arose as a by-product of the material affluence and leisure enjoyed by early civilizations. From these times onwards, selected forms of nature have been isolated from their natural context and experienced within the new setting of an unnatural, intellectually-imposed enclosure. Nature is physically and visually framed within the rectangular bounds of the garden wall. The square of nature thus captured became the garden or "paradise", a word which as *paradeisos* in Greek meant park or animal park, and which was originally derived from the ancient Persian *pairi-daeza*, meaning simply an enclosure. In the gardens of ancient Persia, the right angle was even projected onto the horizontal plane, the garden being divided into four equal parts by artificial watercourses. Attaining "paradise", as we shall see later in a Buddhist context, did not mean getting back to nature as such, but rather to a nature created by man – a garden.

The early Chinese gardens attached to imperial palaces served as hunting grounds. Such gardens were less the object of architectural design than their Near Eastern contemporaries, but were nevertheless enclosed by walls. Here, too, nature was moulded and monitored; even the animals within the park were subject to human control. The ancient gardens of the Near and Far East represented no opposite extremes of "unnatural" and "natural". They differed simply in the type and degree of their artificiality.

The Japanese garden displays this same figurative symbiosis of right angle and natural form in ever new variations throughout the five major epochs of its history. In his seminal essay on Japanese design, Walter Dodd Ramberg expresses his view that beauty is perceived and venerated in Japan either as a property of natural accident or as the perfection of man-made type. In Shintoism, the oldest native Japanese religion, the unique or extraordinary in nature is often venerated as *go-shintai*, the abode of a deity. *Go-shintai* may be an unusually-shaped rock, a tree weathered over the centuries, a strikingly jagged mountain or a waterfall of rare shape or size. In later periods of Japanese history artists made deliberate use of the beauty of natural chance, as revealed in the sophisticated flaws of their pottery glazing and the splashes in their calligraphy.

At the same time, however, the Japanese culture also perceives and pursues beauty in the perfection of the man-made type – in the delicate proportions of the diaphanous paper screen, the wooden lattices on the façades of traditional town houses and the clear linearity of the modular system of classic Japanese architecture. The constructed artefact is viewed as a sort of building set, whose individual blocks are combined according to fixed rules with ever greater functionality

The garden, a piece of "nature" isolated by man:
Toji-in Temple, Kyoto.

and aesthetic perfection. Man's play instinct naturally prompts him to explore and expand these self-imposed systems in ever new permutations.

These two ways of perceiving beauty – as natural accident and as the perfection of man-made type – are not, to my mind, mutually exclusive. Quite the opposite: it is their *simultaneous* cultivation and conscious superimposition that best characterizes the traditional Japanese perception of beauty.

I see this overlapping of the rational and the random, the right angle and the natural form, at all levels of Japanese design: in ornamental tea-house niches (*tokonoma*) hung with scrolls of calligraphy, in a composition of natural, moss-covered rocks viewed through the rectangular frame of a traditional paper

sliding screen, or in a theatrical décor of lions bounding through a bamboo grove which takes up the regular rhythm of the sliding internal partitions below. At their best, these two opposites of random and imposed order complement each other like the Chinese principles of Yin and Yang. Each loses vibrancy if taken separately from the other. Without the contrast provided by a rectangular visual frame or rectilinear background, it would not be possible to recognize a handful of boulders, however carefully selected, as a garden. Thus the "garden" in Japan cannot be treated independently of architecture. The fortuitous order of nature serves to reinforce the rational order imposed by the right angle, and vice versa. In the quest for the perfect fusion – physical and intellectual – of these two opposites, in the quest for a kind of aesthetic *unio mystica*, I see a recurrent motif of the Japanese sense of beauty, one which runs like a hidden thread through the great works of Japanese art right up to the present day.

Perfection of type: the modular order of Kikugetsu-tei Pavilion in Ritsurin Park, Takamatsu. The pavilion was originally built during the Edo era.

Japanese garden archetypes:
The Japanese landscape – Shintoism – Hindu cosmology – Taoist myth –
Buddhist faith – Triadic compositions

Binding trees both shapes their growth and provides additional support for their snow-laden branches in winter. Kenroku-en Garden, Kanazawa (Edo era).
Photo: Minao Tabata

The Japanese landscape: divine islands, divine ponds

kumori naki	Not clouded
yama nite umi no	mountains around the sea
tsuki mireba	in which I see the moon;
shima zo kohori no	the islands, become
tae-ma narikeri	holes in ice

It is difficult to imagine a better portrait of Japan than that painted by this poem, written by the twelfth-century poet Saigyo and perhaps inspired by a view over the Inland Sea. Japan is a country of countless isles in the earthquake belt of the eastern Pacific. Over 70 percent of its terrain is mountainous, with live volcanoes and hot springs, and cleft by deep valleys. The coastline is rocky and fissured, offering only occasional sandy bays. There are almost no flat plains. "Small islands in the sea", "winding rivers between mountains", "rugged rocks along the seashore", "stepped waterfalls" and "pebbles in mountain streams" are all terms in the vocabulary of visual archetypes describing Japan. The Japanese garden employs this same vocabulary; its language of forms reflects that of the landscape of Japan.

It is thus no surprise that the topography of the country should also be reflected in Japanese cosmogony. In the beginning, so the *Kojiki* chronicles of 712 relate, two deities gave birth to eight islands. Only later did they add other natural elements such as the sea, rivers, mountains, trees and herbs. According to Mirei Shigemori, this ancient theory derives from the impres-

can be predicted to within one or two days. The subtle transformations taking place during these periods of natural change are the central themes of Japanese poetry and painting and the Japanese festival calendar. Thus the patterns of kimonos, the flower arrangements in the decorative alcoves of traditional houses, even the type and timing of food served in tradition-conscious Japanese restaurants all reflect the time of year. It is rare even today to receive a letter which does not open with a reference to a seasonal flower or the currently-prevailing humidity or cold.

Although the Japanese garden has, over the course of the centuries, evolved through a remarkable variety of sizes and styles, it nevertheless displays a design logic which is intimately bound up with the *genius loci* of the Japanese landscape – in other words, with the essence of the country as it appears to the human imagination.

Shinto beliefs: sacred archetypes

Permanent shrine buildings appear relatively late in Shintoism; they probably arose during the fifth and sixth centuries AD, when "nature Shinto" slowly entered its second phase of "shrine Shinto". Such was the formal clarity and simplicity of the earliest sanctuaries and the universality of their ritual imagery that they produced specific archetypes of holy site and sacred rite in the collective Japanese subconscious, archetypes which have survived the passage of time and which continue to cast a spell over foreign tourists even today.

sion made by the Japanese landscape on the first settlers arriving by sea. This impression subsequently left a deep imprint upon the collective Japanese subconscious. Man-made recreations of *shinto*, divine islands, and *shinchi*, divine ponds, are found even in the earliest prehistoric shrines, and have proved one of the most fruitful archetypes in the history of the Japanese garden.

Japan has four distinct seasons, and their transition

*Garden attached to the abbot's quarters,
Tenryu-in Temple, Kyoto.*

*The enduring motif of the Japanese sense of
beauty: unio mystica of the right angle with
natural form. Front garden of Honen-in
Temple, Kyoto.*

The earliest Shinto sanctuaries combine different facets of ancient Japanese civilization, such as respect for territorial rights, the worship of nature, the sense of purity and the cultivation of rice.

The territorial archetype: *shime*

The art of knotting and binding was probably one of the first manual skills mastered by the early inhabitants of East Asia. The binding of grasses, bushes and trees was used to signal a personal claim to land or other property. It set a *shime*, a mark of occupation or possession and hence of power. I have already set out, in a number of publications, the complex set of deductions which have led me to conclude that from the archaic Japanese *shime* is derived the Japanese word *shima*, "garden". *Shime* literally means a "bound artefact", which in turn signifies "occupation" (the verb *shimeru* possesses all three meanings). The word *shima*, derived from *shime*, means "land" or, more specifically, "land which has been taken possession of". It later acquired the meaning of "garden", or rather "a section of nature fenced off from the wilderness". It finally came to mean "island", a "piece of land floating in the untamed ocean". In the noun *shime-nawa*, (literally "rope of occupation"), used to describe the ropes delimiting a sacred area or sanctifying a holy object within a Shinto shrine, we find a use of the word *shime* which goes beyond the politico-economic sense of possession as expressed by binding to assume a religio-magical significance.[1]

The Japanese fascination, indeed obsession with binding, manipulating and even crippling plants for gardens or miniature landscapes thus has its roots in a cultural phenomenon dating back literally thousands of years.

The rock archetype: *iwakura* and *iwasaka*

The appreciation of the beauty of natural rock has been one of the most pronounced characteristics of the Japanese garden throughout its history. Rocks are employed in garden composition for their sensory, scenic and symbolic effects, a distinction David Slawson introduced. Many Japanese and Western academics trace this love of pure, unadulterated stone to the worship – possibly dating from neolithic times – of huge boulders and rocky outcrops such as those found in ancient Shinto shrines. These rocks were often bound with the *shime-nawa* ropes mentioned above to indicate their sacred character, as is the case in the Omiwa shrine near Nara. Rocks thus identified are accepted as *go-shintai*, the abode of a deity, leading many to conclude that prehistoric Shintoism must have undergone an animistic phase. It is my opinion, however, that the appreciation of the beauty of rocks, and the worship of a divine presence concealed behind them, is a relatively late phenomenon in the history of Shintoism. Such rocks were originally called *iwakura* and *iwasaka*, literally meaning "rock seat" and "rock boundary", suggesting that they were placed in preanimistic times as markers, denoting occupation of land or property. At

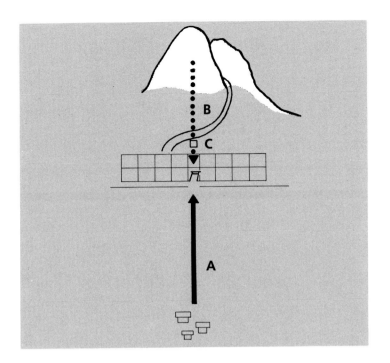

Diagram of the shinden, or Divine Fields, showing both the basic geomantic relationships between mountain, water and ricefields, and the "path" of man (A) as distinct from the "path" of the combined deity of the mountain and paddy fields (B).

some stage their original meaning and function were forgotten, and they acquired religious as well as territorial significance. Later still even similar naturally occurring (not man-made) rock-formations came to be seen as abodes of deities.

Mirei Shigemori, on the other hand, argues that certain unique natural stone and rock formations were considered sacred from the very beginning. To these were added, over the course of time, other rocks, thereby creating a sacred precinct which was at least in part man-made. In the final phase, a particular sanctuary might have all its rocks imported. This marked the beginning of Japanese garden architecture proper.[2]

However different these standpoints, both underline the special status afforded the natural rock in Japan. Castle walls aside, natural stone has never played a major role as a building material in traditional Japanese architecture. On the contrary, stone is finely appreciated for the subtle distinctions of its form, colour and texture, and an individual rock may even be assigned the human characteristics of head and feet, front and back. Rock has thereby acquired archetypal status, and a Japanese garden without an unusual rock or rock group, natural or carved, is quite inconceivable.

The agricultural archetype: *shinden*

The daily offerings of rice and sake which are made to the deity of sun and food in the shrines of the Imperial Ancestors at Ise are prepared from rice specially grown in the so-called "Divine Fields", or *shinden*. These fields represent a last surviving example of Japanese geomancy as it existed prior to its replacement by the Chinese system imported with the first wave of Chinese influence in the Nara and Heian eras. It was the agricultural cycle of rice-growing (introduced in Japan in the Yayoi era, between 200 BC and 250 AD) which, together with the territorial practices described earlier, contributed most to the architecture of the sacred precincts and religious rites of Shintoism.

The geomantic relations between the various elements of the Divine Fields are simple and clear: on one side there is a mountain, from which water flows down to the fields; on the other lies the *torii*, the typical Shinto gate signalling the entrance to a sacred precinct and isolating it from the secular outside world. No attempt is yet made to orient the entire complex due north, as later stipulated by the rules of imported Chinese geomancy. The whole constitutes a kind of first garden, where deity and human being meet. Rice paddies were integrated into the large-scale gardens of the daimyo nobles from the early Edo era onwards, frequently in the form of a magic square – with 3 x 3 squares giving one magic square.

Behind the religious practice of growing and tending sacred gardens lies the belief, found throughout Japan, that the local guardian deities live in the mountains in the winter, from where they are ceremonially fetched in spring and taken to spend the summer in the rice paddies, until being returned to the mountains in autumn, after the harvest.

According to research by Nobuzane Tsukushi into

ancient folk beliefs in the Ise region, the sun deity at Ise was originally believed to descend once a year from heaven to a high mountain peak near the Isuzu river at Ise. From there the villagers carried it down to the valley in the form of a newly-felled tree, and dragged it across the river at the foot of the mountain. The village community then celebrated the arrival of the deity on the opposite shore, with a local maiden serving the deity as priestess and spouse for one night. The earliest place of worship of the deity thus lay at the river's edge, and probably consisted of little more than a tree temporarily installed at the centre of a patch of pebbled ground marked by a sacred rope.[3]

Much has been conjectured about the mysterious *shiki no himorogi*, which we know only to be a sacred precinct strewn with pebbles in which ritual purifications are performed. Such sites are mentioned in chronicles from as early as the eighth century, and can be seen even today in almost every Shinto shrine – there are a particularly fine examples of *shiki no himorogi* in the shrines at Ise.

I believe that the origins of these *shiki no himorogi* lie in those ancient ablution sites on a riverbank where the mountain deity "appeared" to the community of believers for the first time. Pebble beaches or pebbled areas in Japanese gardens are more than mere copies of a natural phenomenon. They are archetypes of the hallowed ground of Shinto theophany.

Rock setting symbolizing Mount Meru (Shumi-sen), the mountain at the centre of the world in ancient Hindu-Buddhist cosmology. Raikyu-ji Temple Garden, Takahashi.

Hindu cosmology:
The mountain as axis mundi

The arrival of Buddhism in Japan led to the adoption of a particularly potent archetypal image from the cosmology of a foreign culture: the image of Mount Meru (*Shumi-sen* in Japanese), the cosmic mountain at the centre of the universe. Representations of this mountain can be found in many Japanese gardens. The earliest written Buddhist sources, themselves based on even older concepts of Hindu cosmology, see the universe as "a single, circular world system surrounded by a mountain range of iron, *cakravala*, from which its name is derived".[4]

Buddhist *cakravala* cosmology exists in a number of forms, varying according to tradition. All, however, appear to share the same central concept of the universe as a circular disk with Mount Meru at its centre. Lying in concentric circles around this *axis mundi* are seven golden mountain ranges and an eighth and last mountain range of iron, the *cakravala*. There are oceans between the mountains; only in the ocean between the seventh mountain range and the *cakravala* are there four islands inhabited by man. A further eight uninhabited islands float in the other oceans. The disk rests on a foundation of golden earth, which in turn floats on water.

It is important to remember that this image portrays the universe as a whole, and not just our own earth. Mount Meru is the axis of that universe; the golden mountain ranges which encircle it denote the various realms of meditation and heavenly spheres.[5] This originally Indian cosmography was taken up by the Japanese garden. Mount Meru can thus often be found as a single, towering rock, sometimes surrounded by subsidiary stones, prominently located within an individual garden. In other cases, the representation of all nine mountains and eight oceans underlies the design of an entire garden. One of the most beautiful examples here is the garden in front of the Golden Pavilion in Kyoto, where the various islands and rocks in Mirror Lake can be seen as an illustration of an originally Hindu concept of the universe.

Touching the soul of the Japanese islanders even more profoundly than the details of Buddhist-Hinduist cosmology was, however, the powerful image of the *mountain* at the centre of the universe and of the *waters* of both life and death. Mountain and water converge in the image of the *island*, which appears in Japanese cosmology – as indeed elsewhere – as the first manifestation of land, indeed of form as such.

The recurrent appearance of the cosmic mountain throughout the history of the Japanese garden points to the resonance which the simplicity, power and beauty of this pre-scientific model of the universe finds in the collective Japanese subconscious. What I have here termed an "archetypal image", Mircea Eliade calls a "symbol". A true "symbol", says Eliade, "speaks to the whole human being and not only to the intelligence". The concept of the island in the ocean is precisely such a symbol.[6]

Just as the ancient civilizations of East Asia built

The crane island (left) and two turtle islands (right) symbolize, here and in various other combinations, the Isles of the Blest. Illustration from a book on garden design from the seventeenth century.

stupas, temples, even entire cities in the shape of the mandala, symbol of the structural principles of the cosmos as a whole, so it comes as no surprise to find this same mandala, with the axis mundi at its centre, inspiring the design of many a Japanese garden.

Taoist myth: The Isles of the Blest

Myths portray our deepest hopes and fears with an archetypal clarity which ultimately accords them greater power over our minds than historical events. History is a record of conscious data; myth speaks from the unconscious, or from the so-called collective unconscious. The fears of old age and death, for example, go beyond the bounds of mere history. Such fears, and the desire for eternal youth, are directly linked to the Taoist myth of the existence of an island of immortality. Man's untiring search for an elixir of eternal youth is reflected in our own times in the images and promises of the cosmetics industry.

According to ancient Chinese myth there lay, somewhere far, far east of the Chinese coast, five islands populated by men and women who had attained immortality and who lived together in perfect harmony. Legend relates that they flew around the lofty peaks of the islands on the backs of cranes. The islands themselves were carried on the backs of giant sea turtles. Two of the islands were subsequently lost, however, following a battle with a sea monster.

The power which this myth exerted for hundreds of years over the imaginations of the Chinese and, later,

Japanese is reflected in the expeditions mounted by the Chinese emperors to find the islands and snatch the elixir of youth from their immortal inhabitants. Around the turn of the first century BC, all such attempts having failed, Emperor Wu decided to lure the immortals to his own palace by building a garden which resembled as closely as possible the mythical isles themselves. Thus he created a large lake containing four islands, all with palaces. On the shores of the lake he constructed a platform, two hundred feet high, from which to communicate with the immortals.[7]

The myth of the Isles of the Blest must have reached Japan even before the introduction of Buddhism, since it is the subject of a reference in the *Nihon shoki*, the Chronicles of Japan from around 720 AD. An entry for the year 478 mentions the son of one Urashima, together with his beloved (who had emerged from a turtle), as having actually reached the Isles of the Blest and visited the immortals.[8]

As history shows, Japan was as captivated by this myth as by the myth of the mountain at the centre of the universe. It became a characteristic feature of Japanese gardens up until the end of the Ero era. It must be said, however, that Japan condensed the five islands of the original Chinese myth into just one, the island of *P'eng-lai*, or *Horai-zan* in Japanese, which was symbolized in Japanese garden architecture as a Horai mountain, Horai island or Horai rock, and at times even as a crane or turtle island. Cranes and turtles thereby became symbols of longevity in their own right; even today, Japanese celebrations such as wed-

dings and anniversaries will always feature the symbol of a turtle or a crane in some form, whether in a painting, flower arrangement or simply origami shapes.

The similarities between the central archetypes of the myths described above inevitably led to their confusion even before they had left China for Japan. The mountain at the centre of the universe in the Hindu-Buddhist myth forms the backdrop to the drama of the quest for Nirvana, the state of eternal peace. The Isles of the Blest at the heart of the Taoist myth become the stage setting for the attainment of eternal life. Despite the parallels between their spatial metaphors, however, their paths to salvation are different: the first follows the path of meditation, the second the path of magic.

Buddhist faith:
The paradise of Amida Buddha

Meditation and magic were not the only paths traced in the architecture of Japanese gardens. A third path, that of devotion, inspired a vision of paradise which found concrete correlation in the pond islands within Buddhist temple precincts.

Mahayana Buddhism speculates that space is divided into ten realms which contain countless numbers of world systems. Some of these systems lie under the influence of specific Buddhas. One such system is *Sukhavati*, or *Jodo* in Japanese, a "Pure Land" under the influence of Amida (Amitabha), a transhistorical Buddha of infinite light and eternal life. It is located, according to this cosmology, at the "provisional limit

of the worlds to the West" in an otherwise "unlimited universe".[9]

To be reborn in Amida's Pure Land after one's death in this world was considered a significant step towards Buddhahood. Belief in Amida and his paradise can be traced back to three Indian sutras, which arose between the second and fifth centuries AD, in which Shakyamuni tells of Amida's vow to save anyone who faithfully devotes their life to him. Shakyamuni then proceeds to give a vivid description of Amida's paradise, where magnificent palaces are set in beautiful gardens of shady terraces and lotus ponds.

The Mahayana Buddhism from which this idea stems is often called the "Great Vehicle" of Buddhism. In place of the arduous meditational practices of other Buddhist sects, it employs "easier" methods such as chant, prayer and the contemplation of images. Perhaps this explains why Pure Land Buddhism has attracted the largest following of all the Buddhist sects in China and Japan. It is only natural, therefore, that it should also have the largest number of temples in Japan. When looked at more closely, however, the models underlying human representations of Amida's paradise reveal themselves to be worldly rather than heavenly in origin. The visions of Amida's Pure Land both as painted on mandalas and recreated in garden architecture bear close resemblance to the royal pleasure gardens of the ancient Middle East. It is probable, therefore, that the mythological Pure Land of the original Indian sutras was based on descriptions of Middle-Eastern palaces; this would in turn explain why the

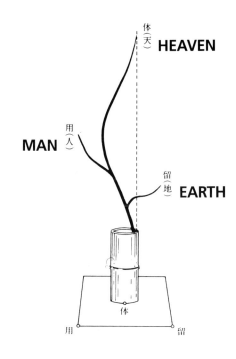

体(天) **HEAVEN**

用(人) **MAN**

留(地) **EARTH**

体

用   留

The triad as archetypal aesthetic principle: in this flower arrangement, vertical, horizontal and diagonal symbolize the relationship between heaven, earth and man.

legendary country lies in the West, and not in the East. The fear of death, as we have already said, runs deeper than all other fears, and goes beyond the bounds of mere history. And thus these last three archetypes of Japanese garden architecture, based respectively on Hindu cosmology, Chinese myth and Buddhist faith, all have one thing in common: they are expressions of man's desire to outwit the laws of nature to which he is subject and to escape death. Paradoxically, man seeks to transcend Nature by means of man-made nature.

Triadic compositions:
The harmonious balance of odd numbers

Arrangements of rocks in groups of three probably date as far back as the gardens of the Nara era. The *Sakutei-ki*, the oldest text on Japanese garden architecture, distinguishes between two different types of such rock compositions: *hinbunseki-gumi* and *sanzonseki-gumi*. The first, *hinbunseki-gumi*, is an arrangement of rocks based on the shape of the Chinese character for "articles", whereby the triadic composition is developed chiefly within the horizontal plane. *Sanzonseki-gumi*, on the other hand, is the name given to compositions recalling sculptures of the Buddhist Trinity. Here the triadic composition is developed within the vertical plane. Such rock triads appear throughout the history of the Japanese garden – both in splendid isolation and as part of a larger sequence, perhaps beside a waterfall or on the banks of a pond.

The significance of these Buddhist-influenced rock arrangements lies not in their religious symbolism but in their aesthetic composition: a large rock in the centre with two smaller rocks on each side. I do not accept the prevalent theory that "aesthetic values generally originate in a religious sphere; they develop and gain autonomy as religious values decline"[10]. It fails to take account of the triad, a deep-rooted archetype of aesthetic composition which was only later adopted by a variety of religious iconographies.

In Japan, the use of three components – one large, one small and one medium-sized – to create a dynamic balance of odd numbers is not merely limited to garden architecture, but lies at the heart of Noh theatre and the art of flower arrangement (*ikebana*). Thus three basic compositional elements of *ikebana* are the "branch of truth" (the tallest), the "accompanying branch" (slightly shorter) and the "flowing one" (the shortest). They are usually referred to as *ten* (heaven), *chi* (earth) and *jin* (man), the archetypal Chinese definition of the tripartite structure of the universe. A later text on garden architecture defines this same compositional archetype as a trinity of forces, one horizontal, one diagonal and one vertical, which correspond to the triad of Heaven, Earth and Man.[11]

The garden surrounding a tea house in Katsura
Imperial Villa, Kyoto. The garden, whose origins
date back to the seventeenth century, represents
a synthesis of Japanese garden architecture.

The Japanese garden in history:
From prototype to type and stereotype

The evolution of religious, artistic and social thinking in Japan is mirrored in the role assigned to rocks and plants by Japanese garden designers. This role has changed greatly over the course of history. It began as the imitation of the external forms of nature, but as the laws of nature became increasingly understood, its focus shifted to the imitation of the essence of nature and its internal mode of operation, only to move on, in modern times, to the superimposition of man's egoistic will on nature.

Each major epoch in the history of the Japanese garden has approached the garden archetypes described in the preceding pages from the standpoint of its own understanding of form and function, with the result that each has given birth to its own new, unique prototype. The development of the formal language of these prototypes was thereby directly related to changing attitudes to nature, to socio-political conditions and to religio-philosophical trends; in short, to the intellectual climate as a whole.

The invention of a new garden prototype and its exploration in various types does not imply a renunciation of the previous prototype; rather, it represents a dynamic reinterpretation and combination of the old with the new. With historical hindsight it is thus often possible to discover the germ of a later prototype still dormant in a much earlier one. At the same time, however, there are inevitable instances of mere mechanical repetition, where gardens simply copy the stereotypes of the past.

With reference to E. Ambasz's "Theory of Formal Types", I see the prototype as the product of the gardener as artist, the type as the product of the gardener as craftsman and the stereotype as the product of the gardener as purely commercially-minded designer.[12]

Sacred islands and ponds
Gardens of joy

The gardens built during the Asuka, Nara and Heian eras clearly reflect the first great wave of Chinese influence to reach Japanese culture. The scenery of the earliest Japanese garden prototype is dominated by islands and ponds. As such it quite literally illustrates the Sino-Japanese word for "landscape", *san-sui*, or "mountain-water". At the same time it reflects the ancient Chinese dual principle of Yin and Yang, in terms of gardening. The Heian garden is large in scale; it is more a seascape than a landscape garden designed to be enjoyed by boating. The later gardens of the Heian period are usually sited within the rectangular framework of the Shinden-style architecture of early Heian palaces and temples of Pure Land Buddhism. Such gardens were generally designed by their noble owners themselves as a setting for courtly festivities, whereby the elements of the garden sought to imitate the external forms of nature.

Kyokusui no niwa, the Garden by the Winding
Stream, dating from the Nara era. Located on the
south-eastern edge of the grounds of the former
Nara imperial palace, the garden was excavated
and reconstructed between 1975 and 1984.
Its pond formed part of a large residential estate
occupied by Nara nobility.

Gardens in ancient Japan

Almost nothing has survived of the gardens of ancient
Japan. Their forms and functions can thus only be infer-
red from a limited number of literary sources, archeolo-
gical excavations and hypothetical reconstructions by
Japanese scholars.

The *Nihon shoki*, the Chronicles of Japan of 720 AD
whose records span a period from prehistoric Japan up
to 697 AD, contains sporadic references to gardens
which, when taken together, add up to a surprisingly
clear picture of the first palace gardens in Japan. Below
is a selection of these entries:

In the spring of 74 AD, so the *Nikon shoki* relates,
Emperor Keiko "resided in the Kuguri Palace and, let-
ting loose carp in a pond, amused himself by looking
at them morning and night."[13] In 401 AD Emperor
Richu had a pond built at his palace in Ihare. In Novem-
ber 402 "the Emperor launched the two-hulled boat
on the pond of Ichishi at Ihare and went on board with
the imperial concubine, each separately, and feasted."[14]
In around 413, the consort of Emperor Ingio was
"walking alone in the garden" when a nobleman on
horseback looked over the hedge and said: "'What an
excellent gardener thou art. Pray, madam, let me have
one of those orchids.'"[15] In 486 Emperor Kenzo "went
to the park, where he held revel by the winding
streams".[16]

In 612 an emigré from Korea faced banishment to
an island because of his flecked skin. Empress Suiko

spared him, however, when she heard his plea that
he could "make the figures of hills and mountains".
Thanks to his remarkable talents, he was subsequently
employed to create a "Mount Sumeru" and a "Bridge
of Wu" in the southern courtyard of the imperial palace.[17] It is thought that this Bridge of Wu may have
been an ornamental bow-shaped bridge such as is
frequently found in Chinese gardens. The shape and
nature of Mount Sumeru remains, however, a mystery.

In 625, during the reign of the same Empress Suiko,
a minister by the name of Soga no Umako – a member
of the powerful Soga clan – owned a palace "on the
bank of the river Asuka. A small pond had been dug in
the courtyard, and there was a little island in the middle of the pond. Therefore, the men of that time called
him *shima no oho omi*, which translates as 'Lord of the
Island(s)'."[18] This palace later passed into the hands of
the imperial family and acquired the name of *Shima no
miya*, "Palace of the Isles". It is mentioned in a number
of poems in the earliest anthology of Japanese poetry,
the *Manyoshu* or "Collection of a Myriad Leaves" which
was compiled in the mid-eighth century.

However fragmentary these literary references, they
nevertheless enable us to piece together a fairly accu-
rate portrait of the first Japanese garden prototype.
The earliest palace gardens were clearly of impressive
size. Why else should a powerful minister be called after his garden? They were located in or near the southern courtyards of royal or noble residences. Their chief
scenic elements included a pond with one or more islands, symbolic representations of an ocean landscape,

together with man-made mountains and a winding stream with rocks placed along its banks.

It is not known precisely where within Fujiwara-kyo, capital of the Fujiwara clan (694–710), or Heijo-kyo, "Capital of the Castle of Tranquility" (710–784), these gardens were located, nor where they lay in relation to the imperial palaces themselves. Only a few such gardens have been excavated, and much remains hypothetical. It is generally believed that the two above-named capitals, with their palaces and Buddhist temples, were modest imitations of the architecture of the Chinese T'ang dynasty. Thus it may be surmised that their gardens, too, were influenced by those of the T'ang, which ranged from huge pleasure gardens, via rock gardens copying mountains and gorges, to the gardens of court nobles and ministers.

552 AD is widely accepted as the year in which Japan began seriously to copy China's far superior culture. Japan's oldest chronicles, the *Kojiki* of 712 and the *Nihon shoki* of 720, both agree that this was the year in which Buddhism officially reached Japan. Together with Buddhism (which was imported from the kingdom of Korea) came the Chinese script and various works of Chinese art. This by no means implies there were no contacts with Korea or China before this date. With time, relations between the Japanese islands and the mainland were strengthened by official missions to the Chinese court. P. Varley writes:

"The Japanese dispatched a total of four missions to Sui China during the period 600–614 and fifteen to T'ang between 630 and 838. The larger missions usu-

ally consisted of groups of about four ships that transported more than five hundred people, including official envoys, students, Buddhist monks and translators. Some of these visitors remained abroad for long stretches of time – up to thirty or more years – and some never returned. The trip was exceedingly dangerous, and the fact that so many risked it attests to the avidity with which the Japanese of this age sought to acquire the learning and culture of China."[19]

This first large wave of Chinese influence left traces in Japanese thought and art which can still be felt today. Sierksma divides acculturation processes into three phases: first, a phase of identification, of simple imitation of the foreign culture. This is succeeded by a phase of reinterpretation and, finally, by a phase of complete assimilation and absorption. I see the Japanese absorption of Chinese culture as following this same progression, whereby the first phase corresponds to the Tumulus (250–552) and Asuka (552–710) eras, and the second to the Nara era (710–794) and the early years of the Heian period. Sierksma writes of this second phase: "Acculturation is always characterized by reinterpretation. Objects and ideas are taken over from the strange culture, but derive their meaning from the context of the old culture within which they are now placed. Or again, indigenous elements of culture are given a new meaning in the context of the new strange culture."[20]

Such regular cultural exchanges with China exerted a profound influence upon the religion, arts, government, economic system and social structure of Japan.

In 894, however, one hundred years after the founding of Heian-kyo, they came to an abrupt end. Japan broke off all diplomatic and cultural relations with China shortly before the collapse of the T'ang dynasty.

This simultaneously marked the beginning of the third phase of the acculturation process, which reached its climax approximately a century later with Japan's complete assimilation of Chinese values and forms.

The Heian period

The gardens and architecture of the Heian period (794–1185) reflect, in the first half of the period, the processes of Japanese reinterpretation of Chinese culture and, in the latter half, the results of its complete assimilation.

In 794, at the command of Emperor Kammu, the capital of Japan was moved to Heian-kyo (present-day Kyoto). It remained in this "Capital of Peace and Tranquility" until 1868, when it moved to Edo, which was in turn renamed Tokyo, "Capital of the East".

The grid layout structuring both the imperial residence and the city as a whole is derived from Heian-kyo's great – and considerably larger – Chinese model, Changan, which was the capital of China under the Sui and T'ang dynasties from 583 to 904. The rules of Chinese geomancy also dictated Heian-kyo's siting and geographical orientation within the natural landscape. The same rules governed the gardens within the imperial palace complex and the palaces of the nobility.

Sino-Japanese geomancy as holistic design theory

As one of the – what we would now view as – unorthodox sciences practised in China, geomancy was most generally known as *feng-shui*, literally "wind-water", or simply as *ti-li*, "land patterns". In Japan this same body of knowledge was called *chiso*, "land physiognomy", or *kaso*, "house physiognomy". Geomancy seeks to determine the most favourable design and location of human artefacts – a house, a grave, even a whole city – within the natural or man-made environment.

Sino-Japanese geomancy is based on a holistic view of the cosmos, in which man is seen as an integral part of nature and its energy fields. It correlates geophysical factors – geographical land forms, climate, magnetic fields – and astral phenomena – movements of the stars, solstices, lunar phases – with the psychosomatic welfare of the human being. We shall be examining this science in some depth not only because it differs considerably from the indigenous Shinto geomancy discussed earlier in this book, but because it was to prove highly significant for Japanese garden design. Indeed, it influenced not only the positioning of artefacts (including entire gardens) in geographical space, but even governed the movement of human beings in time. During the reign of Emperor Temmu, a central government organ was created within the imperial city to supervise Sino-Japanese geomancy. This was the *Ommyo-ryo*, the Office of Yin and Yang. For all its

superstitious overtones, geomancy reflects a profound
awareness of the ecological relationship between man
and the forces of nature.

The logic of Chinese geomancy, of *feng-shui*, is not
easily grasped by the Western mind. Like other branches
of the traditional Chinese natural sciences, it employs
methods of cognition which are best described as *in-ductive, synthetic* or *synchronistic*, if we may borrow
from the terminology of Porkert and Jung. Such proce-
dures are foreign to the Western mind, which employs
causal, analytic and *diachronistic* processes of
thought.[21]

To the uninitiated, Sino-Japanese geomancy appears
to consist of a vast collection of rules and precepts
whose roots can ultimately be traced both to human
fears – fear of the uncontrollable forces of nature, fear
of hostile neighbours – and human greed. But it also
conceals a fundamental acknowledgement of the interdependence of all levels of reality, both natural and
man-made. It recognizes, too, the energetic quality
underlying all reality – a concept unknown to the
Western mind until the advent of modern physics.

The Chinese geomancy introduced into Japan was
itself a complex amalgam of two schools of thought,
one based on more rational cosmology, the other intuitive. The chief instrument of the former was the geomancer's "compass", a condensed image of the cosmos in its spatial and temporal relationships – a sort of
Chinese mandala.

The Chinese geomantic compass was frequently
subdivided into three levels – Heaven, Earth and Man.

It thus reflected the tripartite division of the Chinese
universe. In line with ancient Chinese speculation on
the cosmos, the compass shows heaven as round and
the earth as square. There is a magnetic needle at its
centre. Concentric rings circling this needle relate the
concepts of Yin and Yang, which express the polarity
of all natural phenomena, to the concept of *go-gyo*,
the five evolutive phases of Chinese natural science,
to the eight trigrams and sixty-four hexagrams of the
I-Ching and to the cycles of the Chinese solar-lunar calendar. These correlations apply equally to outer nature
and inner man. Practical geomancy might thus be described as a kind of acupuncture applied to nature, and
acupuncture as as kind of geomancy applied to the human body. In view of this holistic understanding of the
world, it is not suprising that the design of Japanese
gardens was also subject to the dictates of geomancy.

Perhaps the most striking consequence of this cosmology was the fact that the gardens, cities and palaces of China, and subsequently Japan, were all oriented due north. The Chinese believed that all power
was derived from a non-personal Heaven and was
transmitted to earth via the emperor, until he grew too
weak to perform his celestial mandate. Just as the stars
and constellations in the sky appeared to rotate around
the Pole Star – referred to in ancient Chinese texts as
the "Great Heavenly Emperor" -, so on earth all state
and religious affairs revolved around the figure of the
emperor, the Son of Heaven. He was the *axis mundi*
of the earth just as the Pole Star was that of the firma-
ment. Since the Pole Star lies almost due north, the

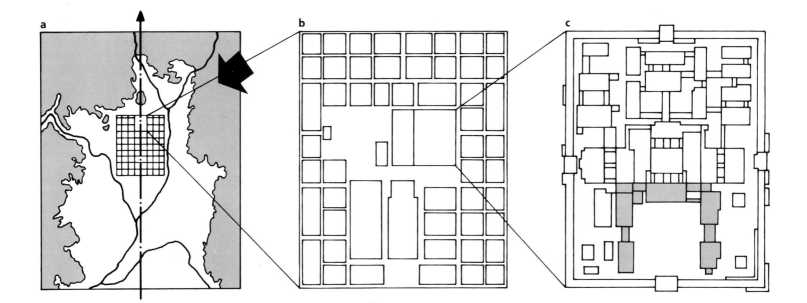

ritually correct position of the emperor was accepted as also being either to the north or at the centre of his capital and palace complex. This cosmological axiom led the Japanese to orient their capital cities, palaces, noble residences, gardens and even the shrine of the Imperial Ancestors in Ise all towards the north.

At the centre of the intuitive school of Chinese geomancy lay the search for an ideal site upon which to build an ancestrial burial vault, a house or even an entire town in harmony with the complex configurations of nature already existing or made by man. The Chinese visualized such ideal locations in the form of a comfortable armchair, its "back" a mountain and its "armrests" hills. In certain cases the "back" might be provided by artificial enclosures such as walls, hedges and buildings. The Chinese word for such an ideal site is *xue*, which means "lair", "den" or "cave", thereby emphasizing its protective function. Significantly, too, the same ideogram represents an acupuncture point in both the Chinese and Japanese languages.

Ideally, the "armchair" will be open and sloping towards the south, and flanked by mountains or buildings on its three remaining sides. These specifications are met both by the old capital of Heian-kyo, which is located within the broad Yamashiro basin (*yamashiro* literally means "mountain castle") and by the *dairi*, the imperial palace within the city itself.

Unlike the cosmological school, however, with its geomantic compass, the more intuitive school had no technical aids to fall back on. Locating ideal sites required instead an intuitive feel for what the Chinese call *ki*, and what M. Porkert translates as "configurative energy", the energy flow within a complex natural or man-made configuration. An intuitive feel for this energy flow could only be acquired through practical training under the supervision of an experienced geomancer.

It is interesting to note that this same concept of *ki* is employed by traditional Chinese medicine, both in diagnosis and treatment. This and other points of similarity have led to the suggestion that acupuncture may have developed out of the historically older science of geomancy. Many of the names assigned to acupuncture points make clear references to geographic and topological features – "bubbling spring", "sea of energy", "small swamp", "bending pond", "inner garden", "outer hill", "receiving mountain" and more besides.

According to the formal school of geomancy, a location is characterized in terms of a dragon. The dragon's "belly" thereby represents the most auspicious site. The contours of the dragon's body are described by mountain ranges and winding rivers, which also represent the components of Yin and Yang. As mentioned earlier, the word for "landscape" – adopted into the Japanese from the original Chinese – is *san-sui*, which means literally "mountain-water". This conceptual and visual differentiation is utterly lost in translation. *San-sui* means the polarity of mountain and water and is one of the most important metaphysical concepts inspiring the formal language of Sino-Japanese garden architecture and its blood-brother, painting.

Opposite:

a: Heian-kyo, present-day Kyoto, was founded in 794. Mountains surround the city on three sides like the back and armrests of a natural armchair. The city opens to the south onto a broad, flat plain. Mount Hiei, Kyoto's highest peak, lies on the far side of the Devil's Gate in the north-east.

b: Daidairi, the palace city, with two large building complexes for state ceremonies in the south and the imperial residence in the centre.

c: Dairi, the imperial residence. The main hall, shishin-den, and the two lateral wings form a man-made armchair embracing an open ceremonial court.

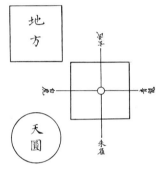

Cosmological school of geomancy. This drawing illustrates the fundamental tenets of geomancy: the earth is square and is surrounded by the circle of heaven; four heavenly animals inhabit the four cardinal points.

School of forms: diagram of an ideal architectural setting, in which an armchair cradles a ming-tang, a bright courtyard.

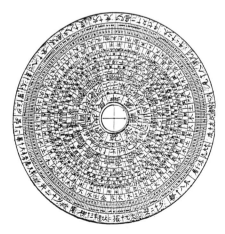

A geomancer's compass. A condensed model of the Chinese universe correlating phenomena of time and space occurring in outer nature and the inner psyche.

Page from an old Chinese geomancer's manual showing an auspicious site within a landscape of mountains and rivers.

35

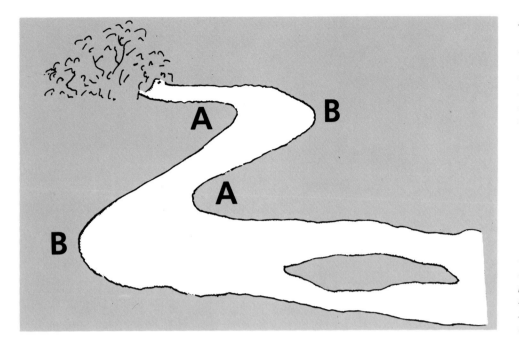

Auspicious (A) and inauspicious (B) sites along a winding river or garden stream. According to the Sakutei-ki, the "Classic of Garden-Making": "The land enclosed within a river bend should be considered the belly of the dragon. To build a house on that belly is to be lucky. But to build a house on the back of the dragon is to invite misfortune."

Right:
Inductive correlations between the five evolutive phases and the four cardinal points, the four seasons, the four mythical heavenly animals, five solid bodily organs and five human emotions. From an old Japanese manual of geomancy.

The geomantic, or better, topomantic location of Heian-kyo is said to have been selected with regard to the mythological heavenly animals residing in the four "corners" of the universe. As writings dating from as far back as the Han dynasty reveal, it was believed that these animals, like all heavenly phenomena, manifested themselves on earth. Thus the Azure Dragon supposedly lived in a mountain stream in the east, the region of morning and spring. The home of the White Tiger lay in the mountains of the west, the region of evening and autumn. Morning and spring thereby represent the time of ascending Yang, while evening and autumn represent the period of ascending Yin. The Black Tortoise was thought to dwell in the mountains of the north, the direction of midnight and winter, while the Red Bird resided in the plains of the south, the direction of noon and summer.

Behind this notion of the four heavenly animals lies the ancient Chinese system of inductive correlations, known as *wu-xing* in Chinese and *go-gyo* in Japanese. Long translated as "five elements", the concept has more recently been rendered as "five activities" or "five evolutive phases". This system originated in the fourth century BC and existed alongside the traditional Chinese notions of Yin and Yang. As the latter represented an understanding of the universe in terms of polar opposites, so *wu-xing* proposed an equally dynamic interpretation of all reality in terms of five phases. These phases were symbolized by the ideograms for earth, wood, fire, metal and water. As shown in the diagram on page 43, the earth lies at

the centre. The four segments of the circle correspond to the four cardinal points, to which are assigned wood (east), metal (west), water (north) and fire (south). Each of these *go-gyo* elements is attributed its own colour: earth is represented as yellow, wood as green, metal as white, water as black and fire as red. As visible in the diagram, these elements are part of a five-stage sequence of concentric circles, and are followed by rings containing the five main bodily organs, five human emotions, the four seasons and four times of day, until finally arriving at the four mythological animals. Everything under the sun found its place within these five stages of transformation, from the five planets and five basic types of animal to the elements of inner man: the five tastes, five voices and five major organs, which in turn correspond to five emotions – anger, joy, sorrow, terror and thoughtful reflection.

This five-phase system of correspondences thus constitutes both a macrocosmograph and a psychogram. It creates continuous cross-references between the outer world of nature and the inner world of man. Even today, the many Chinese pharmacies still practising at a local level in Japan will invariably have on display a chart of these correspondences. A further indication of the importance of this system may be seen in the fact that both the city and gardens of Heian-kyo were laid out in the form of Chinese mandalas, and can thus be interpreted as microcosmic replicas of the universe.

The ancient Japanese belief that evil spirits always come from the north-east, from the *ki-mon*, the Devil's Gate, probably had its roots in a natural phenomenon:

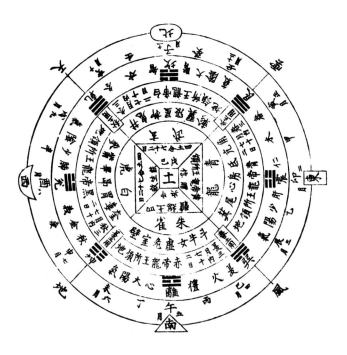

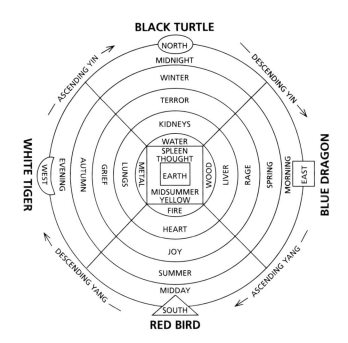

in China and Japan, the bitterly cold winter winds come from the north-east. China furthermore suffered barbarian attacks from this same direction throughout its history, while the hostile and militant tribes who populated the north-eastern regions of Japan were only finally subdued by the Yamato clan. Heian-kyo was safely protected from any such "threat" by Mount Hiei, the highest peak in the armchair of mountains cradling the former Japanese capital and lying exactly north-east of the city.

The gardens of the Heian period may be found in three different types of setting. Some are contained within the palaces of the emperor and the aristocracy and thus fully subordinate to their architectural surroundings. Others are sited on the city outskirts, acting as a kind of intermediary between the urban environment and unspoilt nature. Others still adorn the main courtyards of Pure Land Buddhist temples.

Gardens in an urban palace setting

Nothing today survives of the eighth-century *dai-dairi*, the "great inner interior", as the palace city was originally called. The *dairi*, or "inner interior", as the imperial residential quarters were known, has similarly fallen victim to time. Only the *shinsen-en*, the "Park of Divine Springs" to the south of Nijo castle, lives on as a tiny remnant of the imperial pleasure gardens which once covered an area of 2 x 4 city blocks (260 x 520 yards). According to the historical and literary sources of the day, these pleasure gardens provided the setting for

imperial poetry competitions, banquets and boating trips on the huge artificial lake. The gardens also hosted the *kyokusui no en*, or "Feast by the Winding Stream", a literary event highly popular amongst court nobles. Lining both banks of the winding garden stream, they would compose poems upon a seasonal subject while catching tiny cups of rice wine which were floated downstream.

Gosho, literally "the august place" the present term for the imperial palace in Kyoto is a highly-disciplined form of – originally Chinese – palace architecture. It implies a symmetrical arrangement of successive courtyards aligned along a central axis. In the Heian period this form was invoked not only for palaces but also for Buddhist temples and Shinto shrines, and in particular the shrine of the Imperial Ancestors in Ise.

At the heart of the imperial living quarters lies the *shishin-den*, literally "the purple hall of the Emperor", a word borrowed from the seventh-century *Da-ming* palace complex in Changan. The present *shishin-den* in Kyoto is a nineteenth-century reproduction of an earlier building from the late Edo era. It employs the now-familiar armchair layout, whereby double-aisled covered corridors extend from the main building to enclose a brightly-lit *nan-tei*, or "south garden". Carpeted with white sand, the garden contains nothing but a mandarin tree and a cherry tree, placed at either side of the open steps leading up to the *shishin-den*. Fenced off from the rest of the garden behind a carefully-proportioned wooden lattice, and symmetrically positioned within this ceremonial courtyard, the two

Early hypothetical reconstruction of a palace complex in the Shinden style of the Heian era. This reconstruction by Sawada Nadari, an architectural historian of the late Edo era, was published in his book "Kaoku zakko" in 1842 as the first of its kind.

trees are treated as pieces of architecture rather than as plants in a garden.

The empty and white characteristics of the south garden in front of the *shishin-den* have their origins in the dual function of the early Japanese emperors as both political ruler and chief priest. South gardens were originally reserved for religious and state purposes; empty, they provided a suitable stage for the colourful court rituals borrowed from T'ang China; white, they offered a pure setting for sacred dances performed to invoke the gods.

The cosmological orientation of the whole in accordance with Chinese models is again echoed in the names given to the two side gates leading into the south garden. Thus the *nikkamon*, the "sunflower gate", lies at the centre of the eastern walkway, while the *gekkamon*, the "moonflower gate", is found on the opposite, western side. They recall the temples of the sun and moon found outside the eastern and western gates of many Chinese cities. In Japan as in China, the layout of the imperial palace and its gardens was to reflect the design of the very cosmos itself.

Providing a stark contrast to the formality and austerity of the ceremonial south garden are the *tsubo-niwa*, the small "inner-courtyard gardens" found amongst the rectangular arrangement of buildings north of the *shishin-den*. Intimate in scale, informal and unassuming in character, these are often devoted to one specific plant or plant variety.

The walled garden below the west veranda of the *seiryoden*, the imperial banqueting rooms, is com-pletely flat and almost empty, containing no more than a few simple plants. Garden scholar M. Hayakawa sees this garden as the perfect expression of the Heian sense of elegance and tranquility. I believe it mirrors precisely those motifs I have described earlier as characterizing the Japanese sense of beauty: namely, the play of delicate natural form against the right angle of Japanese architecture, in this case the wooden lattice.

Expanding upon the simple beauty of the *tsubo-niwa* within the architectural maze of the imperial complex, another expert on Japanese gardens, Loraine Kuck, observes: "Ladies whose rooms faced these small courts were often called by the name of the flower dominating them, and this same flower was sometimes also used as a decorative motif in the rooms – stencilled or embroidered onto curtains and screens." Kuck also draws our attention to the name of Fuji-tsubo, the "Lady of the Wisteria Court" who appears in the famous "Tale of Prince Genji"[22].

The Heian nobility, equally concerned to emulate the Chinese fashions of the day, modelled their own gardens on those of the imperial palace. The south gardens of these noble residences no longer consisted solely of empty, sandy surfaces, however; they were joined instead by elaborate gardens laid out to the south, featuring large ponds with one or more islands connected by arched bridges.

The architectural style which dominated the early Heian period became known as *shinden* after the main hall which lay at the centre of palace complexes. It is now generally assumed that the noble residences of

this period were highly symmetrical in their design and occupied a site measuring about 130 x 130 yards (one city block). Two *suiwata-dono*, open corridors, led from the main hall (*shinden*) to two symmetrical side halls (*tainoya*). From there, two covered walkways led southwards towards the pond to a *tsuri-dono*, a fishing pavilion, on one side and an *izumi-dono*, a spring pavilion, on the other. These two pavilions stood right on the water's edge. Halfway along the covered walkways, *chumon* – middle gates – gave access to the inner courtyard. The ceremonial southern entrance gate found in the imperial palace has here disappeared.

Japanese scholar Sawada Nadari, an architectural historian of the late Edo era, was the first to attempt a hypothetical reconstruction of a noble residence in the Shinden style of the early Heian period. I have taken the liberty of reproducing the drawing published in his 1842 "Kaoku zakko" in reversed form, since it thus better fits the description of the winding garden stream found in the *Sakutei-ki*. The *Sakutei-ki* dates from the latter part of the eleventh century and is the oldest surviving text on garden architecture. It contains the clearest description of the first great prototype of Japanese garden: "To ensure good fortune, water must flow in from the east, pass beneath the floor of the house and flow out to the south-west. For in this way the waters of the Blue Dragon will wash away all the evil spirits from the house and garden and carry them to the White Tiger." As already stated, geomantic principles were applied not only to the design of cities as a whole, but also to the palaces and gardens within them. The palace complex was also to be a microcosmic reflection of the universe. The language of the *Sakutei-ki* is full of references to the four heavenly animals and their significance for the building of a house. Thus it writes: "The garden stream should flow into the *shinden* area from the east; it should then be directed south and should leave the garden flowing westwards. Even where the water has to come in from the north, it should be allowed to flow eastwards and then exit by the south-west. According to an ancient sutra, the land enclosed within a river bend should be considered the belly of the dragon. To build a house on that belly is to be lucky. But to build a house on the back of the dragon is to invite misfortune."

By the end of the Heian period, however, the highly formalized, symmetrical architecture of early Heian palaces had been replaced by a freer and more asymmetric style of building. Whether this transition reflected a respect for natural form, or simply an inborn Japanese dislike of symmetry, must remain a matter for speculation. In the new style of the late Heian period, the buildings composing the palace complex no longer stand isolated and independent, but instead flow each into the next. Japan hereby entered the phase of complete assimilation of the Chinese models it had imported in the past, one which Professor Teiji Itoh has termed a phase of "splendid misinterpretations".[23]

On the basis of careful analyses of scroll-paintings, albeit of slightly later origin, historians have been able to reconstruct both the *Tosanjo-den* palace belonging to the Fujiwara clan, and the Hojuji palace built by

Below:
Reconstruction of two noble residences from the late Heian era, revealing a new tendency towards asymmetric design.
Left: Tosanjo-den.
Right: Hojuji-den.
(After O. Mori, 1945, and K. Nishi and K. Hozumi, 1983)

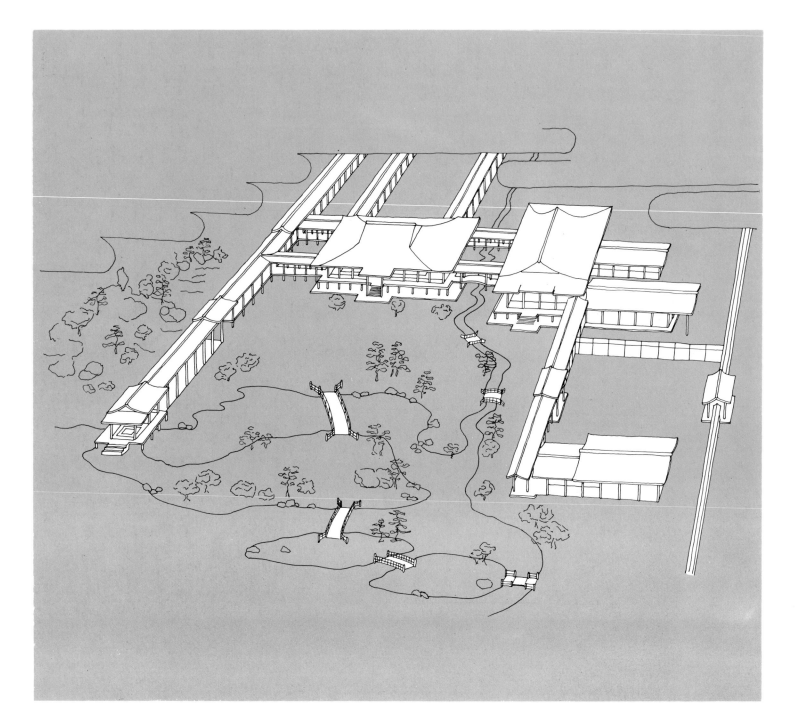

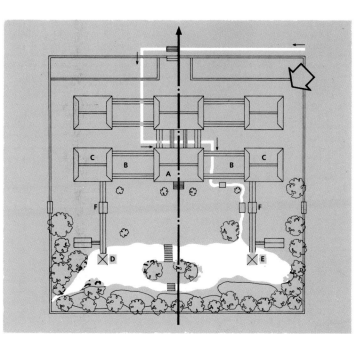

Reconstruction of a palace and garden complex in the Shinden style, whose strong sense of symmetry is a characteristic feature of the early Heian era.
A: Main hall, or shinden, which gave the architectural style its name. B: Open corridors.
C: Symmetrical side halls. D: Fishing pavilion.
E: Spring pavilion. F: Eastern and western gates opening onto the inner courtyard.
(After K. Saito, 1966)

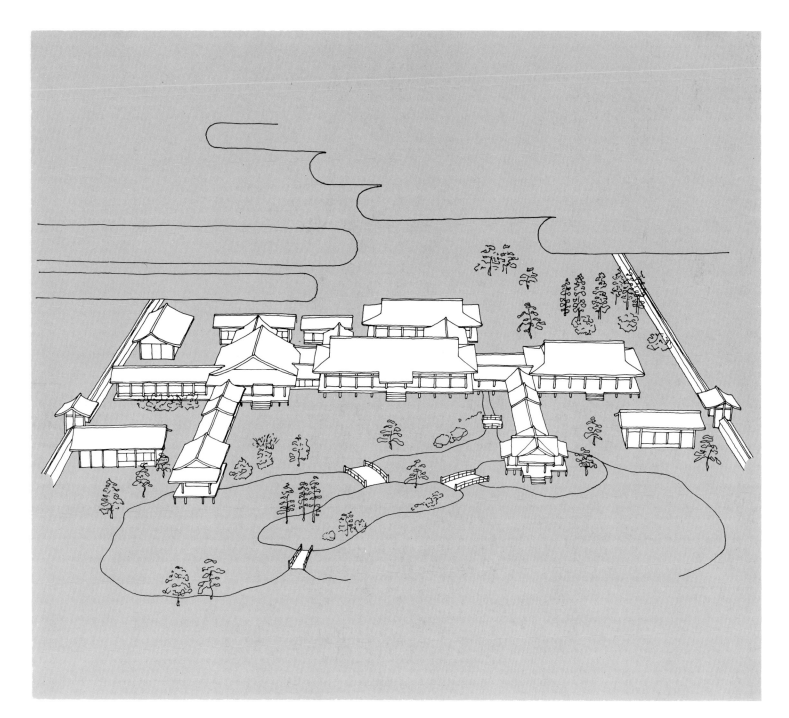

Fujiwara no Tanemitsu (942–992). Their reconstructions suggest that the Fujiwara built palaces of great splendour and impressive size, running the length of two city blocks from north to south. Emperor Goshirakawa chose Hojuji palace as the home of his retirement.

The Fujiwara ("plain of wisteria") clan effectively ruled Japan from the mid-ninth to the late eleventh century from their positions as imperial regents and chief ministers. They guaranteed their continuing influence at court by ensuring that every emperor was the son of a Fujiwara mother. Thanks to their political power and generous patronage of the arts, this period of almost two hundred years has become known as the Fujiwara era.

The Fujiwara continued to design their palaces within the design framework of the "armchair", however asymmetrical the overall composition might now appear. Their gardens, too, were illustrations of that first great Japanese prototype, featuring a pond with one or more islands, its waters fed by a garden stream entering and leaving the grounds in accordance with ancient geomantic rules. The *Tosanjo-den* palace gardens had three islands and one fishing pavilion to the west, while those of *Hojuji-den* contained two islands and two pavilions, one at each end of the projecting covered walkways. The eastern pavilion, built upon a cruciform ground plan unique in Japanese architectural history, stood not on the banks of the pond but on one of its islands, and thus represented a further step away from the clear symmetry of the Shinden style.

In both cases the main hall, the *shinden*, opens di-

rectly onto an empty area of white sand, the site of regular ceremonies and special festivities held on the occasion of imperial visits. Both, too, have garden streams which wind their way through sparsely-planted, slightly undulating ground, and along whose banks that popular banquet of poetry and rice wine, the *kyokusui no en*, was once held. On such festive occasions the islands often provided the location for a *gaku-ya*, a stage for dancers and musicians.

Pavilion gardens on the city outskirts

It had been customary since Nara times for the families of the nobility to build their villas and gardens on the outskirts of the city. Here they could escape the constraints of the urban grid layout and design their houses and gardens with greater respect for local topographical conditions. From the Heian period onwards, these estates became known as *rikyu*, "detached palaces", or *sento-gosho*, "palaces for retired emperors".

One of the few suburban gardens still surviving from these times is Osawa no Ike, literally the "large swampy pond" created by Emperor Saga (809–823) in the north-west of the capital, Heian-kyo. The emperor dammed an existing river to produce a lake with a surface area of some five acres. It formed the central attraction of his detached Saga-in palace in the country, to which he retired after his abdication in 823. In 876 *Saga-in* was converted into a Buddhist temple for the Shingon sect. The temple, called *Daikaku-ji*, can still be seen today.

Saga-in was undoubtedly a palace of outstanding beauty. The elegant right angles of its pavilion architecture and their reflections in the pond must have offered an exquisite counterpoint to the undulating contours of the surrounding landscape. A popular Japanese pastime even today is to sail out onto Osawa pond in early autumn and admire the moon. The ground rises gently towards the mountains to the north of the pond, while flat rice paddies lie to the east, west and south. The northern half of the pond contains the relatively large *benten* island, while the smaller *kiku-shima*, "chrysanthemum island", lies to the east. The charms of this delightful garden inspired poems such as the one below, taken from the *Kokinshu*, an anthology of poety from the Heian period:

hito moto ga	I had thought there was
omoishi kiku wo	but a single chrysanthemum here.
osawa no	Who could have planted
ike no soko	the other one made, there in the
dare ga uheken	depths of Osawa pond?

The size and shape of the pond have changed little over the centuries, although its water level was raised by means of a higher dam in Meiji times, when it was used mainly to irrigate the local rice fields. Most of the rock settings on the banks of the pond were probably washed away as a result. Mirei Shigemori believes that rockwork which he uncovered during excavations in the north of the pond may represent a dry rock waterfall.[24]

This rock waterfall must have been a famous sight in its day, since it forms the subject of a poem in the *Hyakunin isshu*:

taki no oto wa	Though the sound
taete hisashiku	of the cascade
nari nuredo	long since has ceased,
nakoso nakarete	we still hear the murmur
nao kikoe kere	of its name.

Within the precincts of Kanju-ji temple, east of Kyoto, remnants are still visible of the garden which Fujiwara Miyamichi built in the ninth century as part of his palace on the city outskirts. This garden similarly consisted of a pond, probably containing five islands and thus recalling one of the central themes of Japanese garden architecture: the Isles of the Blest.

In a hidden corner of Osawa pond, a lone rock symbolizes an entire island in a faint echo of the architectural vocabulary of the Heian past.

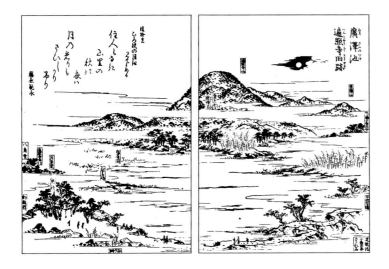

Hirosawa Pond, here seen in a woodcut from the eighteenth century, was built by the abbot Hirosawa in the tenth century as both a garden and a reservoir. The pond remains a popular tourist attraction during the cherry-blossom season even today.

Gardens within temples of Pure Land Buddhism

The urban temple complexes of the Asuka and Nara eras were built around large, open inner courtyards, which functioned as a setting for religious ceremonies and thus paralleled those in the imperial palace used for state ceremonials. Indeed, in the highly formal and symmetrical alignment of its lecture halls, pagodas and corridors, the sacred architecture of these early Buddhist temples largely followed the secular model of imperial Chinese palaces.

The inner courtyards of these early temples were largely devoid of gardens, a situation which began to change as from the middle of the eleventh century, when the Fujiwara princes started funding the building of Pure Land temples inside and outside Heian-kyo. These new temples all included ornamental pond-and-island gardens of the first Japanese prototype category, and sought to emulate the Shinden-style palace architecture of the early Heian period.

In order to understand the temple architecture of the Heian and Fujiwara eras, it is important to consider the underlying mood of the times. There reigned, at least amongst the privileged classes, the feeling of *mujokan*, a sense of the impermanence of the world and of the dreamlike quality of one's own existence. Japanologist Ivan Morris cites a number of images from the literature of the Heian period which reflect such preoccupations. In a poem by lady-in-waiting Akashi addressed to Prince Genji, life is described as *akenu yo no yume*,

a "night of endless dreams"; in another example, the last volume of Murasaki's famous "Tale of Genji" is entitled *Yume no ukehashi*, "the floating bridge of dreams" over which man passes from one life to the next.[25]

This sense of impermanence was largely inspired by the widespread belief that the world had entered the last phase of its history. According to Pure Land Buddhist thinking, humankind had passed through *shobo*, the period of true law covering the first 500 years after Buddha's death, and *zobo*, the period of false law which had lasted the 500 years after that, to reach *mappo*, the period of ending law. It was believed that salvation could only be attained in this final stage through contemplation of the Buddha or by simply uttering the name of Amida Buddha.

This sense of fin-de-siècle gloom, of the futility of all human endeavour, was the inevitable fate of a wealthy society seeking to cure the problem of endless free time with cultural pursuits such as poetry competitions, calligraphy, banquets, semi-religious rituals and state ceremonies, as well as the more physical sports of horse racing, cockfighting and archery. *Mujokan*, the sense of impermanence, and *eiga*, the sense of worldly pomp, are simply two sides of the same coin. But true religion, the understanding of the self, is the greatest luxury of all. Only when man's material and aesthetic needs are met does he become aware of his spiritual deficiences.

Rather than leading to hopeless immobility, however, the worldly boredom and religious despair of the Heian

period resulted, paradoxically, in a blossoming of the arts. It produced some of the finest poetry and novels in Japanese literary history, and some of the most beautiful sculpture and gardens.

The temple gardens of the Fujiwara era were seen as representations of that Pure Land believed to be located somewhere in the West. Just as two-dimensional, painted mandalas of Amida's paradise had earlier taken imperial Chinese architecture as their inspiration, so the architects of the later Heian period similarly looked back to concrete models when composing their three-dimensional mandalas of buildings and gardens. But these models were now the Shinden-style palace complexes of the early Heian period, with their rectangular "armchair" design and pond gardens enclosed within a south garden. Thus the Buddhist temple complex may be seen as a logical continuation of that first Japanese garden prototype. But whereas it was formerly a mere backdrop for courtly entertainments, it now assumed a new, religious significance.

Nothing survives of the early temples of Pure Land Buddhism in present-day Kyoto. A hypothetical reconstruction of Hojo-ji temple suggests that Buddhist complexes shared the same north-south orientation and symmetrical ground plan as the palaces of the aristocracy. Hojo-ji was begun in 1019 by Fujiwara no Michinaga, who is also said to have died within its walls reciting Amida's name. The large temple covered an area of nearly 300 square yards. New to Buddhist temple architecture was the size and position of its Amida Hall, west of the main court, with its eleven bays and nine Amida statues each some fifteen feet tall. New, too, was its pond garden with a central island, housing a stage for religious ceremonies and concerts.

The splendour of the Heian vision of paradise on earth can still be glimpsed outside the former capital in Byodo-in, the "Temple of Equality and Impartiality" built in 1052 by Fujiwara no Yorimichi on the banks of the Uji river. This temple centred entirely around the *Hoo-do*, the famous Phoenix Hall. Inside the Phoenix Hall was a large statue of Buddha; since cosmological considerations required it to face east, the entire complex was in turn oriented east-west. We know from historical sources that the Buddha statue was worshipped from a platform in the pond, the worshipper thereby facing due west, the direction in which the Pure Land of Amida was believed to lie. Musicians would play from decorated barges floating on the waters. The pond itself has changed shape a number of times in its history, but continues to fulfil its original function: to mirror in its waters the elegant symmetry of the temple architecture.

Towards the end of the eleventh century, a northern branch of the Fujiwara clan built a dazzling succession of temples and Pure-Land paradise gardens. The majority lay in Hiraizumi in northern Honshu; all employed the familiar armchair ground plan, in which a garden is cradled by surrounding buildings, and were thus illustrations of the first Japanese garden prototype. Little has survived of these gardens, however. Only Motsu-ji Temple, built by Prince Fujiwara Motohira (died 1157), still preserves something of the original shape of its

"Mystic Island" within the gardens of Kanju-ji
Temple, Kyoto. The temple precincts also
contain remnants of the ninth-century gardens
built by Fujiwara Miyamichi as part of his
residence on the city outskirts.

Heian attitudes towards nature and garden design

Neither the few surviving remains of gardens of the Heian period nor the hypothetical reconstructions of those lost to us provide sufficient bases upon which to judge contemporary Heian attitudes towards nature and garden architecture. We are thus obliged to rely on historical records of the day, of which two literary sources of particular relevance shall be discussed here. The first illustrates the social function of palace gardens, while the second paints a useful picture of garden design and construction.

Genji Monogatari: "The Tale of Genji"

Kisetsu: On living in tune with the seasons

pond and islands. The bold rock settings on its shores are amongst those best preserved from Heian times.

Garden and temple were treated as an integral unit throughout the entire era of Fujiwara temple-building. Over time, however, certain changes nevertheless took place. Whereas the gardens of Hojo-ji temple, which marked the beginning of the great phase of Fujiwara building, are entirely subordinate to the right angle of the temple architecture, the architecture of Motsu-ji Temple, which closed this magnificent era, is entirely subordinate to the design of the garden. The right angle has abandoned its framing function to the garden's powerful embrace.

The "Tale of Genji" represents a pinnacle of indigenous Japanese prose-writing. It was composed just after 1000 by Shikibu Murasaki, a lady-in-waiting. The novel's heroine, who bears the same name as the authoress, supplies both a wealth of observations on elegant Heian court society and astonishingly detailed accounts of the palace gardens and their functions – not least as a setting for romantic encounters.

Japanese art historians have summarized the garden of the Heian period as *chisen shuyu teien*, which translates literally as "pond-spring-boating garden", in other words a garden with a pond whose waters are fed by a spring or garden stream, and which is designed to be enjoyed by boat. If we turn to Chapter 24 of the "Tale of Genji"[26], we find a description of a boating party in Murasaki's spring garden which aptly illuminates this concept:

"Numbers of (Murasaki's) young women who were thought likely to enjoy such an outing were therefore rowed out over the south lake, which ran from Murasaki's south-west quarter to her south-east quarter, with a hillock separating the two. The boats left from the hillock. Murasaki's women were stationed in the fishing pavilion at the boundary between the two quarters.

The dragon and phoenix boats were brilliantly decorated in the Chinese fashion. The little pages and helmsmen, their hair still bound up in the page-boy manner, wore lively Chinese dress, and everything about the arrangements was deliciously exotic, to add to the novelty, for the empress's women, of this south-east quarter. The boats pulled up below a cliff at an island cove, where the smallest of the hanging rocks was like a detail of a painting. The branches caught in mists from either side were like a tapestry, and far away in Murasaki's private gardens a willow trailed its branches in a deepening green and the cherry blossoms were rich and sensuous. In other places they had fallen, but here they were still at their smiling best, and above the galleries wisteria was beginning to send forth its lavender. Yellow kerria reflected on the lake as if about to join its own image. Waterfowl swam past in amiable pairs, and flew in and out with twigs in their bills, and one longed to paint the mandarin ducks as they coursed about on the water."

From this point on they composed poem after poem in an attempt to capture the beauty of the moment. Once back indoors the party continued through the night, with poetry and music-making. Then: "Morning came. From behind her fences, Akikonomu listened to the morning birds and feared that her autumn garden had lost the contest."

The gardens of the Heian period were elegant and colourful, and the festivities held within them were infused with a joyous, light-hearted spirit. They inspired their visitors to express their love of nature through poetry and music. Murasaki's description of the boating party is full of references to the natural signs of spring, and this fascination with the passing seasons is a thread which can be found running through the diaries, novels, poems and paintings of the Heian period as a whole. Anyone who has lived in Japan – and particularly Kyoto – for any length of time will know that spring and autumn are the two seasons closest to the Japanese heart: spring because it is the season in which nature awakens to new life in a burst of fresh and strong colours, autumn for its more subdued rush of yellows, reds and purples and its note of sadness.

Prince Genji tells his favourite lady-in-waiting Akikonumi, whose name literally means "lover of autumn": "But aside from house and family, it is nature that gives me the most pleasure, the changes of the seasons, the blossoms and leaves of autumn and spring, the shifting patterns of the skies. People have always debated the

猫足院乃関白殿、まいらせ給ひぬ事なれ共、小さき人に集りて、のほゝ毎度時座

川にも有者のむ、小なり申まいらせし者、また申させ給しや、御
形の子御とうまさ里申なりたまて、まいらせ小さくても乃へ

法性寺て御はむなれハ、なれんおとて少さてまり乃へ
小ねハは教をも給へとて、左府へ御み、ちかなり
言御かに御童と申きしたつむまれら、小庵つ給

小ため女房こち申あえせて乃、、、御むきされる
子うせ給小むお事なれ共、御子乃ゝりゝ事を

此儀もうゝ見ごにゝ御子乃へ給小左府小
ハ小例有と思へまきて春日大明神つゝせ給小ま

法師乃子我をもて御子乃子にもらゝ御事尾
ゝ小例有と思へますきて春日大明神つゝせ給小ま

まりても、うゝ大将愛小見奈さ乃帮申されに遣人
もらゝ給へて對面し給小左府乃つまやむゝ乃

むゝれたむ里へてゝつつる子我子らやむ
うすゆれ、なき事せうゝらなき村乃子我哉ゝ

て御子と申させち小もら井左まむ毎乃子氏
かまゝ給ちて人いたむせゝゝゝたせられます久

法性寺殿乃御事なる向て、、得、左府乃作
小右大臣顕房ゝ申ゝ人のむを乃え所にむまれ

給うゝ常各也小むこの路て残さゝき尾
里左府々乃事を、いうこゝ忘川やに候給ゝ

ゝ与それよ小乃人をいこゝこよゝゝまおゝゝ
老乃候ふうき眠ぎきれますくゝ卵こ申小乃

うゝれを女君を悉同宿し給ハけら申り大将愛

aware came to acquire an undercurrent of profound melancholy.

Sakutei-ki:
"The Classic of Garden-Making"

The *Sakutei-ki*, the classic manual of garden architecture, provides another inexhaustible fund of information regarding Heian attitudes towards nature and garden design. Japanese scholars consider it probable that the treatise was written in the latter half of the eleventh century by Tachibana no Toshitsuna, a son of Fujiwara no Yorimichi, the builder of *Byodo-in* temple. This attribution would make the author not a professional gardener but a member of the Heian nobility, and probably one who avidly followed – and perhaps actively oversaw – the creation of many a palace garden. The *Sakutei-ki* appears to be simply a compilation of the contemporary rules of garden-making. Whether these rules were already common knowledge and found in other books now lost to us, whether they were passed from teacher to pupil as part of an oral tradition, or whether they were strictly secret, remains a matter of speculation. Nevertheless, the book by Tachibana originally consisted of two scrolls and bore the more appropriate title of *Senzai hisho*, "Secret Discourses on Gardens".

The colophon of the scroll, a tailpiece which traditionally identifies the writer and place of composition, reads: "A foolish old man. This is a very precious treasure; it should be kept strictly `secret'." There is reason to believe, however, that this colophon was only added much later, when the knowledge contained in the scroll had acquired commercial value for a Japanese nobility which had lost most of its power to the samurai warrior class.

At one point in the *Sakutei-ki* the author himself admits: "I have recorded here, without attempting to judge what is good or bad, what I have heard over the years concerning the erecting of rocks. The priest En no Enjari acquired the secrets of rock-setting by mutual transmission. I am in possession of his scriptures. Even though I have studied and understood its main principles, its aesthetic meaning is so inexhaustible that I frequently fail to grasp it. Nor is anyone still alive today who knows all there is to know about the subject. By taking natural scenery of mountains and water, but forgetting the rules and taboos of garden architecture, I fear we will end up with gardens upon which we have forcibly imposed our own forms."

In Heian times, "mutual transmission", like "secret transmission", probably meant simply the passing of knowledge between members of the nobility and Buddhist priests, the two classes of Heian society actively involved in the study and practice of the arts, and particularly garden design. Furthermore, "secret" in a Buddhist context did not mean that a text was physically hidden away, but rather that a "key" was necessary to its understanding. This "key" would be transmitted orally from master to disciple only when the latter was deemed worthy to receive it.

The *Sakutei-ki* discusses garden art and architectural

details within the context of the Shinden-style palace. Sadly it contains no illustrations. The book opens with an introduction to the general principles of garden design, and then proceeds to describe the five types of garden which may be laid out along the banks of ponds and streams. It distinguishes between eight types of island and offers some practical advice on actual construction. The author further identifies nine basic types of waterfall, discusses the various possibilities of garden streams, the different forms of rock settings, and concludes with a jumbled assortment of orally-transmitted dos and don'ts.

The *Sakutei-ki* opens with an excellent introduction to the ground rules of garden architecture in the Heian period:

„The main points to be observed when *erecting* rocks are:

– Design the pond with respect to its position in the land, *follow* its request; when you encounter a potential site, consider its *atmosphere*; think of the *mountains and waters of living nature* and reflect constantly upon such settings;

– When copying the gardens of famous masters of old, bear in mind the intention of your patron and design your version according to your own *taste*.

– When recreating in your garden the *famous natural sights* of other parts of the world, assimilate such *places of beauty* so that they become truly your own. Let your garden express their overall effect. Rocks should thus be erected and harmoniously interrelated."

I have translated the first words of the scroll, *ishi wo tateru*, as "to erect rocks". This literal, perhaps unusual rendering is based on T. Tamura's revised version of the *Sakutei-ki*. Tamura believes that the expression *ishi wo tateru,* and hence the practice of erecting rocks, lies at the heart of Japanese garden architecture of the Heian period. The author of the *Sakutei-ki* himself seems rather baffled by the concept, and observes: "It is generally speaking rare to erect rocks. Rocks are usually laid. We do not seem to use the phrase `to lay rocks' in Japanese, however." I see this as just another example of the very concrete and direct language of historical texts. Abstractions such as "landscape", "scenery" or even "garden" were not yet common currency in Heian times. Instead, words which described a concrete, central activity within the garden-making process were used to denote garden design as a whole. *Ishi wo tateru* is thus used in other contemporary Heian sources as a synonym for garden architecture *per se*.[30]

The elements within a garden are not seen as inanimate objects but as beings with their own character and even their own faces. The *Sakutei-ki* states: „When erecting rocks you should first carry big and small rocks into the garden and assemble them at one spot. Then you should place the standing rocks head upwards, and the lying rocks face upwards, and distribute them across the garden..."

The design principles discussed within the *Sakutei-ki* fall into two types, reflecting two parallel attitudes to garden architecture. The first type are principles imported from China; they clearly reflect the relatively

Rock compositions from the Heian era:
Hokongo-ji Temple, Kyoto. Mirei Shigemori
dates the building of this waterfall, over 12
feet high, to 1130. The style of the waterfall is
described in the Sakutei-ki as tsutai-ochi,
meaning "stepped".

Motsu-ji Temple, Hiraizumi. The point at
which the garden stream flows into the pond
is marked by a number of large rocks on the
shore.

枯
山
水

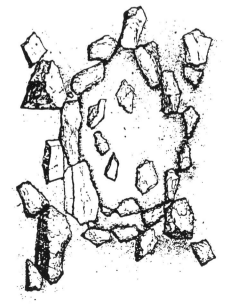

Kamakura or Muromachi eras but simply as the extension of an existing garden type. The *Sakutei-ki* states:

"There are cases where rocks are placed in settings where there is no pond or stream of water. This is called *kare-sansui*. In this type of dry mountain-water garden, part of the hill is shaped like a cliff or undulating landscape, on which rocks are then placed. Should you wish to recreate the scenery of a mountain village, you must provide a high mountain near the main building. You should then place rocks in a stepped fashion from the summit to the foot of the mountain, so that part of the mountain appears to have been removed in order to erect the building. Rocks which are thus excavated in real life have a wide, deep base. Hence it is impossible to extract and remove them from the site. One column of the building should therefore be made to rest on or beside one such stone."

According to contemporary accounts, Zen master Muso Kokushi took over Saiho-ji temple in 1334 and turned it into a Zen monastery. *Saiho-ji* originally meant "westerly temple"; by modifying its ideogram, although without altering its pronunciation, Muso Kokushi changed "westerly temple" to "temple of western fragrances". He had a number of new buildings constructed within the complex; their own architecture, together with the corridors connecting them, must have superimposed upon the gardens outside a rectangular grid through which the viewer inside saw nature. Sadly, none of the original temple buildings have survived.

Japanese art historians differ as to whether the dry

rock arrangement in the upper part of Saiho-ji Temple Garden was indeed created by Muso Kokushi, just as it remains unclear whether the garden represents the new prototype of a Zen garden or the logical extension of an already existing, relatively minor Heian model. Whether the dry landscape garden is solely and exclusively the brainchild of a Zen mind will no doubt equally remain a matter for debate. What can be said, however, is that Saiho-ji Garden arose under the supervision of a Zen priest who was deeply interested in gardening, and that as a product of the Kamakura era it stands, stylistically and chronologically, halfway between the typical Pure-Land paradise garden of the Heian era and the most austere gardens of the Muromachi period.

In Saiho-ji, unlike later Muromachi temple gardens, the visitor is still invited to discover the beauties of the garden in the course of a leisurely stroll along the path around the lake and across the small bridges to the islands.

In the hillier part of the garden, the soft, undulating carpet of moss is interrupted by three extraordinary rock compositions which have fascinated Japanese garden lovers throughout the centuries. The first is the *kame-shima*, a "turtle island" group of rocks floating in this case not in a pond of water but in a sea of moss. Slightly higher up the slope lies the *zazen-seki*, a flat-topped meditation stone suggesting the silence and calm which accompany meditation. The third and last of these famous attractions is the *kare-taki*, a dry waterfall again composed largely of flat-topped granite

stones in a stepped arrangement. Not even a trickle of water travels its rocky course, yet it seems to roar louder than the fullest cascade. So, too, the academic voices debating the historical origins of this dry rock waterfall are drowned beneath the overwhelming beauty of its presence.

Tenryu-ji: the Temple of the Heavenly Dragon

The gardens of *Tenryu-ji*, the "Temple of the Heavenly Dragon", stand, like *Saiho-ji*, on the threshold of a new epoch. *Tenryu-ji* was built on the former site of a country villa belonging to the powerful Emperor Gosaga, commonly known as *Kameyana dono*, the "Mansion of the Turtle Mountain". The grounds of this enormous residence just outside Kyoto extended from the Oi river to the Arashiyama hills, an area much loved even today for its beautiful cherry blossoms in spring and its glorious autumn colours. Gosaga moved to the villa in 1256 following his official abdication. From here he was to continue his unofficial rule for another forty years, until he was eventually forced to flee to the Yoshino mountains, where he died in exile.

Ashikaga Takauji, the man who had ousted him and seized supreme political power, nevertheless feared the avenging wrath of Gosago's spirit. By way of appeasement, therefore, he built a Zen temple within the grounds of the imperial palace. As abbot of this new Tenryu-ji temple he appointed none other than Muso Kokushi, builder of *Saiho-ji*.

Muso Kokushi thus once again supervised the con-

version of imperial quarters and pleasure gardens for Buddhist use. It seems unlikely, however, that he was responsible for the garden's central waterfall and its outstanding rockwork. Compared to those credited to Muso Kokushi in the *Saiho-ji* dry garden, these Tenryu-ji rock arrangements could not be more different. Japanese art historians see them as the first evidence of the foreign influence of the artistic techniques of the Sung dynasty. And although there is still no agreement as to their designer, it is not impossible that the hand behind these compositions was in fact Chinese.

While the pond in Tenryu-ji's garden still contains water, it is clearly too small for the boating parties and large-scale festivies of the Heian era. A path around the pond and small stone bridges crossing miniature ravines instead encourage the visitor to explore the charms of the garden on foot. Despite the replacement of the original buildings by more recent Meiji architecture, the scale of the garden can still be recognized as tailored to that of the *hojo*, the abbot's quarters. Thus the garden is best seen from the *hojo*, whose rectangular architecture frames the garden like a huge, three-dimensional painting.

The landscape painting of the Chinese Sung dynasty exerted a strong influence not simply on the rock compositions around Tenryu-ji's waterfall, but indeed upon the design of the garden as a whole. One of the major concerns of Sung landscape painting was to evoke spatial depth; Tenryu-ji Garden seems to aim at this same compositional effect. When viewed, as described above, "framed" by the porch of the abbot's quarters,

the garden presents itself in a succession of three horizontal planes. The first and lowest is the foreground
strip of sand between the porch and the edge of the
pond, the second contains the pond and rock compositions in the middle distance, and the third and top-
most plane captures the mountain in the background,
in a conscious "borrowing" of distant scenery called
shakkei. The vertical layering of these planes creates
an impression of receding space and thus achieves the
same depth of ground as a Sung-dynasty painting.

Layering as a means of creating an illusion of depth
is employed in other parts of the garden, too, as for example in the *ryumon no taki*, the Dragon Gate waterfall. Viewed from the small stone bridge directly before
it, the – by Heian standards, unusually high – waterfall
presents itself as a tiered sequence of steps. The so-

phistication of its rockwork is similarly suggestive of
Chinese landscape painting. The "carp stone" halfway
up the waterfall – a stone in the shape of a carp attempting to leap up to the next level – is a clear borrowing from the motifs of Chinese art. In China, a carp
passing the Dragon Gate was a metaphor for a student
successfully passing the qualifying examinations for government service.

C.A.S. Williams writes: "The carp, with its scaly
armor, which is regarded as a symbol of martial attributes, is admired because it struggles against the current, and it has therefore become the emblem of per-
severance. The sturgeon of the Yellow River are said to
make an ascent of the stream in the third moon of
each year, when those which succeed in passing above
the rapids of the Dragon Gate become transformed

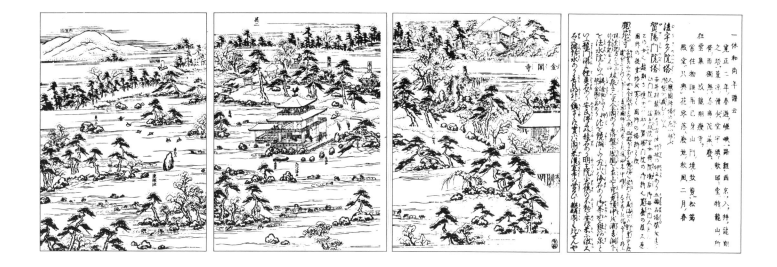

into dragons; hence this fish is a symbol of literary eminence or passing examinations with distinction."[32]

Directly in front of the waterfall, a bridge of three flat stone slabs leads to a narrow path, which in turn passes across a miniature ravine spanned by a single stone. Art historian Wybe Kuitert sees clear evidence of Chinese influence both in the course of this path, with its varying widths and bordering rocks, and in the miniature ravine over which it passes directly opposite the main building.[33]

Tenryu-ji betrays further influence of the garden architecture of the Chinese Sung dynasty in the island group of seven rocks towering out of the pond near the waterfall. In what is probably the finest arrangement of its type in the entire period, these seven rocks symbolize the Isles of the Blest. The bold combination of carefully-selected rocks poetically evokes the soaring peaks of these mystical isles.

The *Saiho-ji* and *Tenryu-ji* temple gardens each point the way forward to a new style in Japanese garden architecture – Saiho-ji with its dry waterfall and flat *zazen* meditation stone, *Tenryu-ji* with its islands, bridge and waterfall inspired by the compositional techniques of Sung-dynasty landscape painting. Common to both gardens is their increasing abstraction of natural scenery. In this they foreshadow the new garden prototype of the Muromachi era.

Palace gardens of the Kitayama and Higashiyama shoguns

Kinkaku-ji

Both the layout and rockwork of the *Saiho-ji* and *Tenryu-ji* temple gardens were to provide models for the palace gardens of the Ashikaga shoguns, rulers concerned to emphasize their cultural interests just as much as their political power. They collected Sung paintings and other works of Chinese art and were seen as active patrons of "modernism". They were keenly interested in the newly-arrived Zen Buddhism and, following their abdication of political and military power, took to retiring to palatial villas outside the city in order to live the monastic life. As variations upon the Heian pond-and-island prototype, however, the gardens accompanying these shogunal villas are far too lavish in both their overall design and individual detail to pass for the austere retreat of a Zen monk.

Kitayama dono, the "Villa of the Northern Hills" dating from Kamakura times, was originally built by Saionji Kintsune in the Shinden style. It was subsequently converted in the early 1390s into a personal retreat for shogun Ashikaga Yoshimitsu, who renamed it *Rokuon-ji*, "Temple of the Deer Park", after the famous deer park near Benares where Gautama Buddha delivered his first sermon after his enlightenment. Today the palace is called *Kinkaku-ji*, the "Temple of the Golden Pavilion", a name inspired by the gilded roofs of one of its pavilions. The golden pavilion which can be seen today is a rebuilt version of the original, destroyed by fire in 1950.

This elegant, three-storeyed wooden pavilion is clearly based on models from southern China. The ground floor comprises a reception room for guests, the second floor a study and the third a private temple for *zazen* meditation. While the open plan of the ground floor looks back to the Shinden-style palaces of the Heian era, the bell-shaped windows on the top floor herald a new style, that of Zen temple architecture.

Although a small path winds its way around the pond, the garden was designed to be appreciated from the water rather than on foot, as revealed by contemporary records of the boating parties and festivities organized in honour of Emperor Gokoma-tsu, who visited the garden in 1408. The garden could also be admired from the three storeys of the Golden Pavilion, from where it was framed within a rectangular architectural structure of harmonious proportions. The pond is subdivided into an inner and an outer zone. The inner zone lies directly in front of the lavishly-decorated pavilion, virtually cut off from the outer zone by a large peninsula and the pond's main island. The outer zone contains just a few small rock islands; its banks are lined with stones. To the viewer in the pavilion, this outer zone appears to lie a great distance away. Directly in front of the Golden Pavilion to the south lie small-scale versions of the traditional turtle and crane islands. Opposite the small boat jetty to the west are two larger turtle islands of particular iconic significance: the "arriving turtle", whose rock head looks towards

the pavilion, and the "departing turtle", who faces away from it.

Two springs rise at the foot of the hills to the north of the Golden Pavilion, each marked by rock compositions. The Dragon Gate waterfall nearby features the legendary carp stone inherited from the original Kamakura garden built by Saionji Kitsune. After Yoshimitsu's death, the palace complex which had been his home in retirement was converted into a Buddhist temple.

Ginkaku-ji

Yoshimasa (1435–1490), grandson of Yoshimitsu, was installed as the eighth Ashikaga shogun when still a child. Even as an adult, however, he took no particular interest in military and political matters, but proved instead a generous patron of the arts. In the course of the bloody Onin Wars which razed Kyoto and its beautiful palaces to the ground, Yoshimasa handed the reins of power over to his son and retired to devote himself wholeheartedly to the construction of his hillside retreat. This *Higashiyama dono*, "Villa of the Eastern Hills" as it was known in his lifetime, subsequently became the centre of cultural life in Japan. After Yoshimasa's death, the villa-palace was converted into a Zen temple, called *Jisho-ji*. The temple is more popularly known as *Ginkaku-ji*, the "Temple of the Silver Pavilion". We do not know, however, whether the name simply reflected wishful thinking on the part of Yoshimasa or whether the pavilion was indeed silver-

The pond and islands of Ginkaku-ji Garden recall earlier Heian prototypes. Behind the senkei-hashi, or Judas-tree bridge, lies the togudo, the Hall of the Eastern Quest, which contains one of the oldest surviving examples of a room in pure Shoin style.

*Inner zone of the pond in front of the Golden
Pavilion.*

*Carp stone in the ryumon taki, the Dragon
Gate waterfall at the foot of the hill to the
north of the Golden Pavilion.
Photo: Ken Kawai*

The Golden Pavilion in the hills north of Kyoto was built about 1394 by Ashikaga Yoshimitsu, and formed the centre of Japanese culture until Yoshimitsu's death in 1408.

plated in emulation of its gilded predecessor built some 80 years earlier.

Yoshimasa, like Yoshimitsu before him, found the inspiration for his new pavilion in *Saiho-ji*, the "Temple of Western Fragrances" – albeit interpreting his model very differently to his shogun grandfather. The Silver Pavilion was based on the *ruri-den* which Zen master Muso Kokushi has conceived as part of the Saiho-ji complex. In contrast to the three-storeyed Golden Pavilion, the Silver Pavilion has only two floors, and houses a statue of the Buddha of Compassion on the second floor. The ground floor, which commands a magnificent view of the garden beyond, was used for meditation.

The division of the garden into two parts is also taken from *Saiho-ji*. Thus the lower section contains a garden for strolling centred around a pond, while the steep slopes of the upper section reveal a dry rock garden.

Of the twelve buildings which originally composed *Ginkaku-ji* temple, the Silver Pavilion and a hall containing a statue of Amida Buddha are the only two to have survived into the present. It is thus no longer possible to appreciate the gardens in their original setting. It is nevertheless clear that here, too, nature was intended to be viewed through, or offset against, the rectangular framework of wooden temple architecture.

The lower part of the garden, with its pond and islands, remains a variation upon the earlier Heian prototype, although its winding paths and stone bridges now encourage strolling rather than boating. The origi-

nal plan nevertheless included a boat-house. One of the garden's chief attractions is its *sengetsu-sen* waterfall, the "spring in which the moon washes". It was clearly intended to capture the reflection of the moon "washing" itself in the waters.

The *Ginkaku-ji* we see today is a mere shadow of the temple which Yoshimasa had originally planned. But building was still unfinished at his death in 1490, and the palace subsequently fell into dispair. Decay was compounded by looting, and it was not until the early seventeenth century that restoration work was begun.

Two specific aspects of *Ginkaku-ji's* gardens foreshadow the mature form of the dry landscape garden of the late Muromachi era. The first is a dry rock arrangement closely resembling that of *Saiho-ji*. It is located on a steep hillside in the upper part of the garden, near the *ocha no i*, the "tea water well". The second is the fact that, for the first time in the history of the Japanese garden, the topographical elements of ocean and mountain are symbolized solely with sand. Thus the ocean is represented by *ginshanada*, literally "silver sand open sea", an area of white sand raked to suggest the waves of the sea. The "mountain" rising from its centre is the *kogetsudai*, "platform facing the moon", a cone of sand recalling the shape of Mount Fuji. These two features would have been highly unusual for a garden of Yoshimasa's time and it is uncertain whether he actually planned them himself. No reference to them is found until a hundred years after his death, in a poem composed by a Zen monk at *Tenryu-ji* temple in 1578.[34]

Ryoan-ji, a supreme example of the beauty of empty space and the interplay of right angle and natural form.

the purpose of meditation. Its overwhelmingly horizontal composition invites the arriving visitor to sit and contemplate it at leisure. Indeed, the word "sit" in Japanese is a synonym for "meditation".

I have found no records to confirm what nevertheless remains my strong suspicion, namely that the composition of the Ryoan-ji rock-and-sand garden has its roots in a Zen meditational technique of staring at a fixed point. Since only in the rarest cases will art and architectural historians have been trained in such meditational techniques, they are inevitably barred access to the secrets of *Ryoan-ji*.

Zen has always adopted a very scientific approach to meditation. It thereby contrasts greatly with our Western philosophy and its mind games, and our Western religion based on "blind faith". Zen starts with fact. And the most obvious and immediate fact in the life of every individual is their body. Consciousness lies at the centre of the body, the senses at its boundaries, and other objects beyond it. Meditational techniques serve to divert man's energy from flowing outwards towards other objects to flowing inwards towards his centre. In *Ryoan-ji*, objects (the rocks) are so perfectly arranged in space (the raked sand) that the viewer eventually ceases to experience them separately. Outward energy reverses to inward energy as the viewer's concentration now turns to focus upon his own consciousness. This is the "experience" of nothingness, of the void, emptiness, impartial awareness, "self-lessness", as we can only inadequately describe it. It is not a philosophical concept but a notion deriving from personal insight.

"Consciousness has turned in upon itself; the circle is complete. You have come home." [40]

But the empty expanse of sand in front of a Buddhist temple or the blank piece of paper in Zen painting is not in itself sufficient to inspire such profound insights. It needs the sophisticated interplay of form with its non-form, of object with its space. It is here, perhaps, that we find the ultimate purpose of garden art – to provide the necessary forum for such insight. The garden of *Ryoan-ji* symbolizes neither a natural nor a mythological landscape. Indeed, it symbolizes nothing, in the sense that it symbolizes *not*. I see in it an abstract composition of "natural" objects in space which is intended to induce meditation. It belongs to the art of the void.

Daisen-in

Daisen-in, the "Great Hermit's Temple", is one of the sub-temples comprising the extensive *Daitoku-ji* temple complex belonging to the Rinzai sect of Zen Buddhism. Situated in the north of Kyoto, *Daitoku-ji* was begun in 1326 by Daito Kokushi, Zen master and contemporary of Saiho-ji designer Muso Kokushi. *Daisen-in* itself was founded within the grounds of *Daitoku-ji* by Kogaku Shuko in 1509. The garden was probably completed at the same time as the main hall in 1513.

Karl Hennig has undertaken a detailed analysis of the authorship of the various elements of the garden. He concludes that the earliest section, centering around the turtle and crane islands, was probably the

The raked sands of the garden south of the main hall, with the Bodhi tree in the far left-hand corner.

work of Kogaku Shuko himself, perhaps with contributions from *sensui kawaramono*, the riverbank workers who had now become gardeners. Soami, the celebrated painter who executed the monochrome seasonal and Chinese landscapes on the sliding doors of the main hall, may also have had some influence on the garden's design.

The main hall, *hondo*, is surrounded by garden on all four sides. The *hondo* itself is oriented along a north-south axis which divides the building into two rows of three rooms. It is a ground plan which was to prove typical of the early Shoin architecture of the Muromachi era.

The garden was designed to be "read" from north-east to south-west. This is also the direction followed by the dry "river", which thus consciously or unconsciously obeys the old Heian rules of geomancy. The powerful austerity of Daisen-in is unsurpassed amongst Zen gardens. Unlike *Ryoan-ji*, however, its symbolism is clear and easy to grasp. Taken at the simplest level, it is a dry mountain-waterscape garden which employs a rapid succession of small scenes to describe a highly abstract landscape within a limited space. Thus the famous L-shaped north-east garden is a representation of Mount Horai and its rivers. Mount Horai takes the form of a clipped camellia, from which there gushes a "spring" of white gravel. This plunges over a "waterfall" and branches into two ever-widening "rivers". One of these flows westwards, past a turtle and baby-turtle island, into the northern garden, called *chukai*, whose white-gravelled surface symbolizes the "middle

sea" of its name. The modest size and enclosed nature of this northern garden recall the courtyard gardens of earlier palaces. It contains one of Japan's most outstanding triadic rock compositions.

The second of the "rivers" flows past numerous rocky obstacles and over a dam before finally converging into the large garden on the south side of the *hondo*. In the south-western corner of this empty expanse of white gravel stands a lonely Bodhi tree, the tree under which Gautama Buddha is traditionally related to have reached enlightenment. This Bodhi tree is a clue to the garden's deeper significance.

The garden is in fact a symbolic representation of the course of human life. Thus the river of life springs from the lofty heights inhabited by the immortals, plunges joyfully down the cascading torrent of youth and into maturity. It now follows a more sedate course along which the trials of adulthood are accompanied by a broadening of experience. The rocks in the path of the river symbolize the hard lessons of life. Thus, in the second garden to the east, we find a rock in the shape of a treasure boat, floating with the current, just beside a stone in the shape of a turtle floating against the current. The first represents the wealth of experience that comes with old age, the second underlines the futility of seeking to oppose the flow of time. The river of life ends with the experience of the void symbolized by the expanse of white gravel in the southern garden. The final hurdles to be overcome have now softened from rock into two cone-shaped mountains of gravel.

The garden can be appreciated at deeper levels again,

in esoteric interpretations accessible only to adepts of Zen. Here the rocks become the difficulties encountered in the search for the answer to that most fundamental of *koan* – "Who am I?". (A *koan* is an insoluble Zen riddle used as a meditational exercise along the road to enlightenment. – Translator's note.)

Seen from an art-historical point of view, *Daisen-in* Garden is unique in the fact that it links for the first time the themes of the original Chinese Horai myth with the austerity of a dry landscape garden. It is similarly unique in its combination of a large number of rocks of varying shapes, sizes, colours and textures within a very small space. Here as before, the forms of nature are perceived through the rectangular structure

of the temple and against the boundary garden walls, in an aesthetic interplay paralleled in the physical juxtaposition, in *Daisen-in* closer than anywhere else, of "built" and "painted" landscape. Whereas *Ryoan-ji* offers the viewer a garden which is composed frontally, like a painting, in *Daisen-in* the visitor is surrounded on all sides by a garden which is both painting and architecture at once.

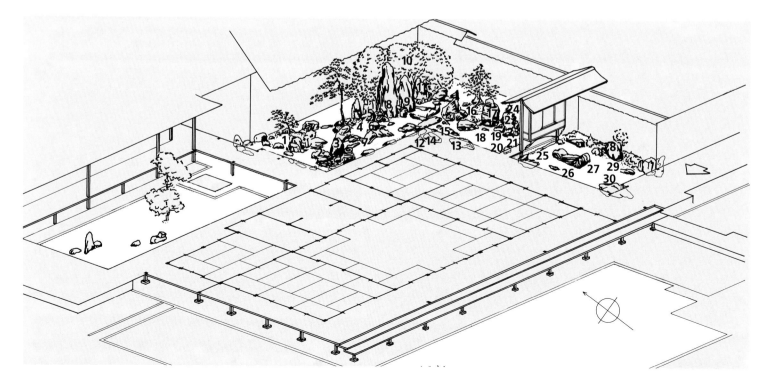

94

Senshu-hashi, the Bridge of the Hermit's Sleeve composed of two stone slabs in Ginkaku-ji Temple.
Photo: Ken Kawai

Shinju-an

Shinju-an, the "Pearl Hermitage", lies just east of *Daisen-in* as another of the sub-temples comprising the *Daitoku-ji* temple complex in Kyoto. It was founded under its present name in 1491. Karl Hennig has again made a detailed study of the various theories put forward by Japanese scholars as to the possible authorship of the garden, and concludes that it was probably created by the poet Socho at the start of the sixteenth century.[41] A second theory links the garden's design with the name of tea-master Murata Juko (1423–1502) – a man who was in turn closely connected with Ikkyo Osho (1394–1481), an enlightened master and probably the leading figure in the arts of his day.

The garden to the east of the abbot's quarters is a dry landscape garden in elongated form. It is covered with moss, not sand as in the garden of *Ryoan-ji* temple, and fenced in by a low, clipped hedge rather than a wall. The numerical and formal arrangement of fifteen moderately-sized rocks along a slightly curved axis in a ratio of 7:5:3 is similar to *Ryoan-ji*. It departs from the tradition of locating such gardens south of the *hojo*, however, and resembles instead the narrow east garden of *Daisen-in*. History relates that it was originally possible to see Mount Hiei over the hedge, whose silhouette would then have been part of the overall garden experience.

In contrast to *Ryoan-ji* and *Daisen-in*, *Shinju-an* draws attention by its very lack of pretention. Such is its quiet modesty that many would never suspect there was a garden here at all. I would again beg to disagree with those who see the garden in terms of islands floating in the sea. To me it represents a highly abstract, rhythmic composition of natural rocks on an available oblong space. It delights our sense of beauty by this very simplicity. Like notes on a musical score, the rocks sound against the geometric trim of the hedge and within the visual frame of the pillars and eaves of the *shoin*. The grouping of its rocks in the ratio of 7:5:3, a harmonious means of distributing an uneven number, is found in gardens from Muromachi times on. To dismiss it simply as cosmological speculation, imported to Japan by Zen priests returning from Sung-Dynasty China, is to ignore the significant role played by the numbers 5 and 7 as metrical measures in Japanese poetry from its earliest origins.

Muromachi attitudes towards nature and garden design

Changes in thematic inspiration, authorship and architectural setting

We have now examined three variations of the second great Japanese garden prototype, all intended to illustrate the unique nature of the *kare-sansui* dry landscape garden developed during the Muromachi period. *Ryoan-ji* is an abstract rock-and-sand garden attached to the south of the abbot's quarters, *Daisen-in* a highly symbolic garden of rocks, sand and plants surrounding the main temple hall on all four sides, while *Shinju-an*

Tenryu-ji is probably the first garden in the
history of Japan deliberately to exploit landscape
elements lying beyond its boundaries. This
"borrowing" technique is called shakkei.

is a thin strip of rock-and-moss garden east of the abbot's quarters. The gardens of the Muromachi era are much smaller in scale than their Heian predecessors; they also reveal fundamental new developments in the areas of thematic inspiration, authorship and architectural setting. In identifying the nature and origins of these changes, we shall be examining the roles played by landscape painting, *sensui kawaramono* gardeners and Shoin-style architecture.

The role of landscape painting

In the figure of Sesshu (born c. 1420), Japanese painting finally progressed beyond the mere imitation of artistic models imported with the second wave of Chinese influence, and reached that final stage of acculturation in which absorption is so complete as to allow new and original departures. Sesshu nevertheless visited China to undergo further training in the techniques of ink landscape painting. The art of the Sung and Yuan dynasties had slowly filtered through to Japan with the arrival of Chinese Zen priests, who came to settle in Zen temples in Kamakura from the mid-thirteenth century onwards.

Art historian Ichimatsu Tanaka mentions an early "Catalogue of Treasures of Butsunichi-an" compiled by the monks of the sub-temple of *Engaku-ji* in Kamakura, and concludes: "Judging by the examples of Sung paintings in the catalogue, however, it is reasonable to assume that Sung influence was already manifesting itself in the Japanese painting of the time."[42] These paintings were initially devotional in character, and included portraits of famous Zen priests or Buddha figures in a landscape setting.

The first independent ga-in, a type of art academy, was founded in the mid-fifteenth century under the Ashikaga shoguns. Many of its members were priests and painters residing in Shokoku-ji, one of Kyoto's five most important Zen temples. Josetsu, first head of the academy, and his successors Shubun and Sotan quickly established a distinct Muromachi style of suiboku, Japanese ink painting.

Sesshu had also been a monk in Shokoku-ji. But having trained at this remarkable dual institution of Zen temple cum art school, he broke away from its institutionalized traditions in his forties to begin an independent career, leading the life of an itinerant monk and painter. His rejection of the conventions of Chinese-inspired landscape painting is a symbolic indication of Japan's increasing cultural independence. Tanaka offers the following summary of Sesshu's achievement: "He thus represented the vanguard in a natural trend towards artistic independence as painting progressed from the religious to the purely aesthetic."[43] Perhaps "natural" would be even better than "aesthetic", for Nature herself is now Sesshu's religious theme. Nature in his work is no longer the mere backdrop to devotional portraits of Buddhist saints, no longer the idealized setting of a Pure-Land paradise, but acquires its own religious significance. Sesshu's perception of nature clearly reveals the influence of Zen on his work: he accepts nature as "religious" iconography. The

words attributed to Zen monk Dogen (1200 –1253) here spring to mind, in which he compares "the sound of the valley and the colour of the mountains" to the "tongue" and "body" of the Buddha.[44] The later Zen priest and painter Hakuin expressed a similar belief when he said: "This very place the Lotus Paradise, this very body the Buddha." The dualistic vision of Heian times, in which the present world of suffering was compensated by the paradise of Amida Buddha beyond, has here given way to the non-dualistic Zen vision of the Muromachi era, in which sacred and profane, matter and spirit, Buddha and ordinary mortal are seen as a single whole.

It is interesting to note that Sesshu was simultaneously a practitioner of meditation, painting and garden design. Although conclusive evidence remains lacking, he is credited with the creation of a number of gardens in western Japan. If, as we have already suggested, he indeed approached his painting as a form of religious exercise, then we may infer that he saw garden design in a similar light.

I would finally like to draw attention to Sesshu's particular preference for splashed and dabbed brush strokes, a technique which he learnt in China. It is possible that he selected rocks with a view to achieving similar textures in his gardens.

The gardens of the Muromachi era are thus no longer the scenic illustrations of nature recommended by the Sakutei-ki in Heian times. They are related instead to a new school of painting whose own origins lie in the religious practices of Zen Buddhism. And like

paintings, they are designed to be viewed statically. The Heian *chisen shuyu teien*, the pond-spring garden designed to be enjoyed by boat, has given way to the Muromachi *chisen kansho teien*, the pond-spring garden designed to be enjoyed from fixed vantage points. At the same time, too, the waters of the first pond garden have effectively evaporated into the "dry" ponds of the latter.

The gardens of the Muromachi era are thus three times removed from nature. Firstly, because they are "constructed" like a landscape painting; secondly, because they are designed to be seen from a distance; thirdly, because they offer an increasingly monochromatic representation of nature, as found in Chinese landscape painting.

The role of *ishitateso* and *kawaramono*

Who were the people who actually designed and built the gardens of the Kamakura and Muromachi eras? In Heian times it seems they were mainly designed by their owners, members of the nobility, as a form of aesthetic pastime. This thesis is supported by an anecdote from the *Sakutei-ki*, the "Classic of Garden-Making". The author of the *Sakutei-ki*, Tachibana Toshitsuna, was himself a noble and a garden-maker, and there is surely a hint of sympathy in the following account: "When the repairs to the *Kaya-in* buildings were finished, all those who were to erect the rocks disappeared. Even those who had just come along by chance and who had been thought capable of the job

failed to satisfy the master's wishes. Fujiwara Yorimichi therefore completed it all himself."

The above passage implies two things. Firstly, that the aristocrat and garden-owner Fujiwara Yorimichi designed his garden himself. Secondly, that even in Heian times there existed a class of professional gardeners whose services could be bought. If so, who were they?

An important key to our answer lies in the form of the *Sansui narabini yakei-zu*, a seminal text transmitting the illustrated secrets of garden design. It was composed in 1466 in *Shinren-in*, part of the *Ninna-ji* temple complex belonging to the Shingon sect in northwestern Kyoto. Ninna-ji had become known as a centre of *ishitateso*, "rock-setting priests" who combined their Buddhist duties with garden design. It seems it was they – and no longer the nobles themselves – who created many of the gardens of the Kamakura era.

As years went by, so interest in gardening increased, a development encouraged by the willingness of the shoguns to promote the newly-imported Zen religion. By the early Muromachi era, what was once the province of semi-professional *ishitateso* had become the domain of Zen priests. The most famous of these was Muso Kokushi, whose name is linked with *Saiho-ji* and *Tenryu-ji*, two of the most famous gardens of the age, and who is even credited by some with the invention of the dry landscape garden *per se*. Priest-cum-gardener Sesshu even brought a third qualification to his work – that of painter.

But alongside the nobility, the Buddhist priests and the Zen painters, there were others involved in the

making of Japanese gardens who came from the opposite end of the social spectrum. These were the
kawaramono, or "riverbank workers", social outcasts
forced to live on the narrow riverbanks because it was
the only land that nobody owned. They earned their
meagre living from labouring work and from such de-
spised tasks as the butchering of animals, abhorred for
religious reasons by the rest of society.

These kawaramono were initially brought in, virtually
as forced labour, for physically-demanding tasks such
as earthworking. They were also required to find and
collect rocks and trees for new gardens from all over
the Kyoto region. Over time, however, their work must
have taught them a broad spectrum of knowledge and
a wealth of valuable gardening skills; by the fifteenth
century they had earned the admiration and esteem of
the Ashikaga shoguns, themselves avid garden build-
ers, and their social status was correspondingly high.
One of the most famous of the sensui kawaramono,
the "riverbank workers as gardeners", was Zenami. The
suffix "ami" indicates that he belonged to the Jishu
sect of Buddhism, whose thirteenth-century founder,
Ippen Shonin, commanded particular popularity
amongst the "common people". Zenami is credited
with the execution of Yoshimasa's "Villa of the Eastern
Hills", the present-day Ginkaku-ji. He died in 1482 at
the age of over ninety, highly respected by the shoguns
for his unique talents as a garden designer and builder.

Karl Hennig is probably correct in assuming that the
new garden prototype of the Muromachi era was „invented" between 1433 and 1471, and thus during

Zenami's active career as a professional garden architect.[45] But whether the dry garden landscape is the intellectual property of the kawaramono, the Zen priests,
the priest-painters or indeed even of the shoguns
themselves, remains a matter of speculation.

Shoin-style architecture and the hojo garden

The Kamakura and Muromachi eras saw political
power in Japan pass into the hands of the samurai, the
warrior class which supplied the shoguns of the day.
The focus of cultural life correspondingly shifted away
from the palaces of the formers emperors to the residences of the samurai and the Zen monasteries which
they sponsored. The garden was equally affected by
these changes, and its scale, social function and architectural environment were all modified accordingly. The
transition from the shinden-zukuri residential architecture of the Heian palace, with its ceremonial south and
pond gardens, to the shoin-zukuri architecture of the
Zen temple, with its garden in front of the hojo, the
abbot's quarters, was a long and gradual process which
lasted until late into the Muromachi era.

During the Kamakura and Muromachi eras, the
Japanese copied both Chinese Zen thinking and Chinese Zen architecture. Daitoku-ji and Myoshin-ji, two
temples built for the Rinzai Zen sect in Kyoto, are
clearly based on Chinese models. The core architectural
components (entrance gate, lotus pond, main gate,
Buddha Hall, Lecture Hall, bathhouse and toilet) are
strictly aligned along a north-south axis at the centre of

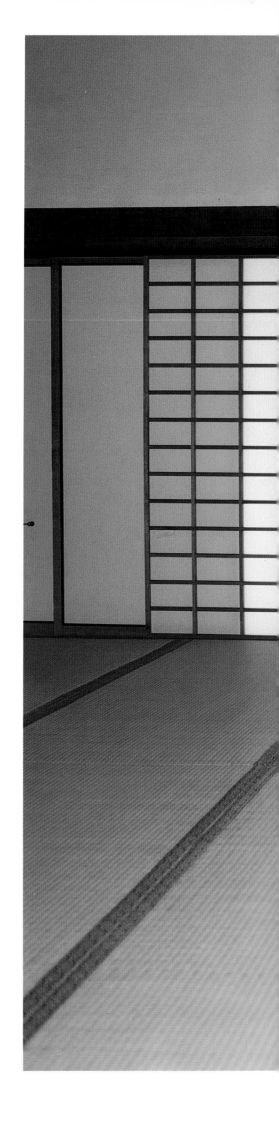

Joza no ma, the main audience hall in Kojo-in
Guest Hall, is a classic example of fully-devel-
oped Shoin-style architecture. A typical feature
is the bay projecting out into the garden; it
contains its own decorative alcove (tokonoma)
and built-in wooden writing desk (tsuke-shoin)
from which the garden can be contemplated.
The polychrome painting on a gold background
in the decorative alcove shows a waterfall and
garden stream, whose waters appear to flow
out towards the garden; Shoin and garden are
thus fully integrated.

the temple complex. Around them, in less disciplined arrangement, lie numerous sub-temples. The abbot's quarters lie to the north of the central complex. The sub-temples were founded by eminent individual monks; they enjoyed a large degree of financial and organizational autonomy, and were also surrounded by high walls which separated them from each other and from the main temple – all features distinguishing them from their Chinese forebears. It was here, in the small courtyards created by the unsystematic addition of individual sub-temples, here in front of the *hojo* and the *kyakuden*, the Guest Hall, that the garden of the Muromachi era found its new architectural setting.

An important catalyst in the slow crystallization of Muromachi *shoin-zukuri*, literally „writing-room architecture", was the *kaisho*, the Assembly Hall designed to house festivities and other gatherings. The *kaisho* first appeared during the Kamakura era, when it employed the Shinden style of Heian palace architecture; it was used by the new military aristocracy for cultural events such as banquets, poetry, tea ceremonies and flower arranging. It was usually located to the north of the *shinden* main hall, in other words in the most private part of the palace complex.

The two great authorities on Shoin architecture, Teiji Itoh and Fumio Hashimoto, both agree that the changes first introduced in the *kaisho* "acted as a force drawing the whole of residential architecture towards the Shoin style as it was eventually formalized in the late sixteenth century."[46]

The following were to become typical features of Shoin-style architecture, although not necessarily all are found in its early phases in any one single building:

Tsuke-shoin, a low wooden desk built into an alcove, with a window overlooking the garden, which was used for reading and writing and which gave its name to the style as a whole.

Tokonoma, a built-in alcove designed to receive flower arrangements and small objects of art. Vertical-hanging scroll paintings imported from China were particularly popular.

Chigaedana, a combination of asymmetrical shelving and cabinets which housed books and valuable tea utensils. These were also usually imported from China.

Chodaigamae, a set of painted sliding doors offering the master of the house a convenient means of leaving and entering the *shoin*.

Other important elements of Shoin-style architecture were its sliding wall partitions. Those indoors were called *fusuma* and were solid and often decoratively painted, while those separating the inside of the house from the garden outside were called *shoji* and were translucent. These partitions could be easily slid aside to allow a view of the garden from indoors. The garden became to some extent a framed element of Shoin architecture. This proved a characteristic of samurai and priestly residences.

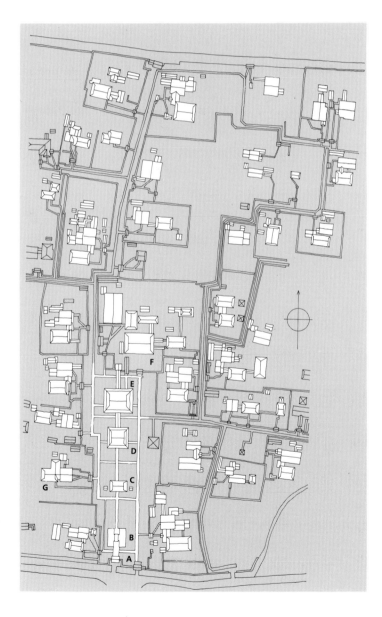

Overall plan of Myoshin-ji, one of Kyoto's large Zen temples, built during the Muromachi era. The core architectural structures are aligned in strict symmetry along a north-south axis. A: Entrance gate; B: Lotus pond; C: Main gate; D: Lecture Hall; E: Buddha Hall; F: Abbot's quarters; G: Taizo-in sub-temple. The remaining areas are sub-temples loosely grouped around the main temple.

Aesthetic ideals of the Muromachi era and their influence on garden design: monomane – yugen – yohaku no bi

In the opinion of garden expert Mirei Shigemori, the *kare-sansui* garden reflects two aesthetic ideals fundamental to Muromachi thinking: *yugen*, a profound and austere elegance concealing a multi-layered symbolism, and *yohaku no bi*, the beauty of empty space.[47]

For Shinichi Hisamatsu, a scholar of aesthetics, gardening is just one of several forms of art inspired by Zen Buddhism. Hisamatsu has identified seven characteristics peculiar to all of these arts; these now famous qualities make a thought-provoking list:

Asymmetry
Simplicity
Austere sublimity or Lofty dryness
Naturalness
Subtle profundity or Deep reserve
Freedom from attachment
Tranquility

The ultimate aim of all Zen disciplines is to help mankind to see its "original face". This, man's true nature, is the formless state of "no-self". Hisamatsu therefore concludes that the problem posed by needing to achieve "the expression in form of the Self without Form necessarily produced the aforementioned singular group of arts that necessarily possess these Seven Characteristics."[48]

Wybe Kuitert, and to a lesser extent Karl Hennig, suspect that the small medieval *kare-sansui* garden has

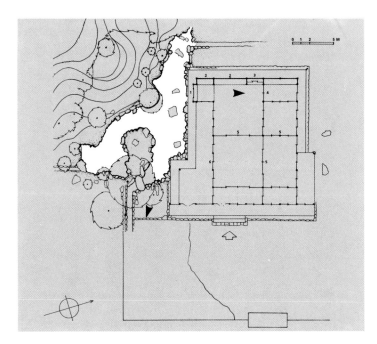

only acquired the label of "Zen art" in more recent times. It is a label which has gained currenty in particular through the work of D. Suzuki, Kitaro Nishida of Kyoto University and Shinichi Hisamatsu mentioned above, all from the twentieth century. For Kuitert, however, the Muronachi garden has other origins: "its composition as well as aspects of its appreciation derived ultimately from Chinese landscape art." Further on he writes: "For the time being, the word Zen can only seriously be used with regard to medieval garden art when it indicates cultural inspiration by Sung or Yuan China. The question remains then whether it should be called Zen."[49]

Kuitert's doubts may be justified. But the fact remains that even China's Sung and Yuan cultures were heavily influenced by Zen Buddhism. It is also a fact that the most important dry landcape gardens on the Muromachi era were almost all built within Zen temples.

In the *kare-sansui* of the Muromachi era I see the garden artist seeking to imitate nature at a newer, deeper level. The transition from the Heian to the Kamakura/Muromachi garden is one from "feature-oriented landscape" to "quality-oriented landscape", as David Slawson terms it, whereby the two need not be mutually exclusive.[50] The Heian garden imitates the outer forms of nature within a selective landscape of natural features. It seems to me that the Muromachi garden takes a step further: it seeks to imitate the inner forms of nature and thereby fathom the secret laws of its proportions and rhythms, energy and movement. Its

means a abstract compositions of naturally-accurring materials. Nor is there anything "unnatural" about such compositons; after all, their rocks came directly from nature, where they would have remained unseen but for the detective eye of the designer.

Zeami (1363-1443), father of the classic Noh theatre and a contemporary of the architects of the *kare-sanui* garden, was the first to systematically expound the notion of *monomane,* the "imitation of things", in the Japanese arts. In a theoretical treatise he describes the initial aim of the Noh actor as being "to imiate all objects, whatever they may be".[51] Imitation is thus seen as *the* means of penetrating beneath the surface of reality.

Once the actor has succeeded in imitating objects, the next step is to identify himself with them as completely as possible. "In the art of imitation there is a realm called 'non-imitation'. When the actor pursues his art to its ultimate and truly grows into the object, he will not be aware of his art of imitation," says Zeami.[52]

Only then can he express *yugen,* that much-disputed concept from the aesthetic vocabulary of the Muromachi era. *Yu* means "depth" and "darkness", gen "profundity", "darkness" and "sublimity". *Yugen* thus suggests an elegant beauty concealing profound depth, a beauty which lies within rather than without, and as such is tinged with the fundatmental sadness of all evanescent life.

Zeami's theory sees the ultimate in Noh acting as being the ability to express "super-natural" beauty in

what Zeami terms the "style of a profound flower". This hidden beauty, which goes above and beyond the superficial beauty of nature, I see in the gardens of such as *Ryoan-ji* and *Shinju-an*.

Another feature common to both Noh theatre and the Muromachi garden is their multi-layered symbolism. "Symbol," according to Max Bense, "means substitution. A number or a word is a symbolic sign which signifies its designatum independent of any morphological correspondence or real relations."[53] Thus the meaning of a symbol is not obviously apparent; it must be learnt.

In *Daisen-in*, water is substituted, or symbolized, by white gravel. This same "water" is itself a symbol of the river of life and the progress of a Zen adept. The themes of the *kare-sansui* garden are not the changing seasons and natural sights of the Heian era, but the inner secrets of nature and human existence. The scenery, too, tends towards an abstract composition of volumes, spaces, textures and rhythms. The naming of rocks, as we shall see later, is equally a means of symbolizing deeper meaning.

Another feature distinguishing the *kare-sansui* from its Heian predecessors is the space it leaves empty. It is a development paralleled in the illustrated scrolls of the Kamakura era: whereas the parchments of Heian times were crammed with detail, generous areas were now assigned to nothing but mist, cloud or simply bare sky. For the Japanese, such new paintings and gardens displayed *yohaku no bi,* the beauty of empty space. *Yo* denotes "remainder" and *haku* "white". It is a feel-

ing common to the Zen garden, the relatively large, unpainted spaces in Zen painting, the moments of silence in Noh music and the phases of stillness in Noh dance.

Highly appropriate to our context are the words of Shinkei, the fifteenth-century poet who emphasized the stylistic importance of empty space in poetry thus: "In linked verse, put your mind to what is not". His thoughts clearly echo those of Zeami in his famous statement on Noh theatre: *Senu tokoro ga omoshiroki* – "What (the actor) does not do is of import."[54] For the Western, non-Zen viewer, the art of *yohaku* is perhaps best described in terms of Mies van der Rohe's "less is more"; the less that is made explicit, the more that is left to the imagination of the beholder.

Sansui narabini yakei-zu: an illustrated treatise on garden landscapes

The *Sansui narabini yakei-zu*, like the *Sakutei-ki* before it, is a text which emphasizes the importance of the secret oral transmission of the arts of gardening. It dates from 1466 and was compiled by Shingen, one of the *ishitateso* priest-gardeners affiliated to Ninna-ji Temple in Kyoto. Although some of its information still pertains to Heian garden prototypes, the *Sansui narabini yakei-zu* – which might be translated as "An illustrated manual of forms of mountain, water and field landscapes" – is chiefly concerned with the smaller medieval garden in the Shoin-style setting. In contrast to the *Sakutei-ki,* Shingen's text is accompanied by explanatory drawings. Two themes in particular recur through-out the book, the first concerning the cosmic laws governing rocks, the second the names given to rocks. Both indicate that the symbolism attached to man-made rock formations in the Muromachi era was becoming more complex.

The first of these themes is introduced right at the start of the text, where it is expressly stated that rock settings should follow the dictates of Sino-Japanese geomancy, the interaction of Yin and Yang and in particular the laws of the five evolutive phases. The text says:

"Bearing in mind the Five Colours of Rocks, you must set them with full consideration of the relationships of Mutual Destruction and Mutual Production. In the cycle of Mutual Destruction, Wood destroys Earth, Earth destroys Water, Water destroys Fire, Fire destroys Metal and Metal destroys Wood. Let this be your guide. A person of the Wood nature has blue-green for his colour, so you should not set a yellow rock in the direction he faces, since Wood destroys Earth..."[55].

Since the Sino-Japanese science of the Muromachi era classified virtually every natural phenomenon between earth and heaven in terms of the five evolutive phases, it comes as no surprise to read that rocks, too, had their own place in the system. They were categorized in terms of colour, size, shape and texture, and their placement was governed by cosmic laws. Hence individual rock settings became more than simply imitations of famous natural sights or metaphors of mountains and islands within a garden; they now

expressed the energetic constellations of nature. They offered the garden-maker a symbolic language in which to state the more profound truths of nature which lay beneath its aesthetic surface.

The second recurrent theme of the *Sansui narabini yakei-zu* is the naming of rocks. The book abounds with what at first sight appear rather apocryphal rock titles. Some – "Never-Ageing Rock", "Rock of Ten Thousand Eons", "Rock of Spirit Kings" – recall the Chinese Taoist myth of the Isles of the Blest. Others, such as "Hovering Mist Rock", "Boat-Concealing Rock" and "Bridge Anchoring Rock" describe particular scenic effects. "Crescent-Configuration Rock" and "Erect and Recumbent Rock" communicate sensory impressions. When given a name, natural objects – which in themselves have no meaning – acquire an individual significance. Garden scholar David Slawson has made a meticulous analysis of the names of rocks, categorizing them in terms of "scenic effects", "sensory effects", "cultural values" and "geological habitat"[56]. To my mind, however, such analysis is too scientific, too rational for its subject; gardens, after all, have never been designed by purely rational methods alone. Slawson's separate categorization of scenic effects, sensory effects and cultural values also strikes me as highly questionable, since I believe our ways of perception and interpretation are inevitably conditioned by our culture. For me, the naming of rocks is simply an indication of the increasingly symbolic dimension of the gardens of the Muromachi era, in which human interpretation is superimposed onto natural garden scenery.

Rocks composing a dry waterfall in Ichijodani
Valley, north-east of Lake Biwa.
Photo: Katsuhiko Mizuno

*Rocks around a former pond with islands in
Ichijodani Valley.
Photo: Katsuhiko Mizuno*

A bridge of natural stone, 34 feet long, links the turtle and crane islands in the dry landscape garden of Senshu-kaku, which lies below Tokushima Castle on the island of Shikoku.

new perceptual dimensions which they opened up were to precipitate recognizable changes in the design and layout of Momoyama gardens. A typical example is the pond garden immediately to the north of the *oku no shoin*, the innermost *shoin* of Taga Taisha Shrine in Shiga Prefecture. The garden, a product of the early Momoyama era, contains what were originally two islands (now two peninsulas), a dry waterfall with a bridge of natural stone in front of it and rocks representing *Shumi-sen* (Mount Meru) and Mount Horai. What is striking, however, is the fact that the entire garden lies some nine feet below the level of the *shoin,* and must therefore be viewed from above.

Senshu-kaku

This new type of Momoyama garden, dominated by outsized rocks and sunken ponds – features which say more about the vainglory of their owner than about the secrets of nature – finds outstanding expression in the garden of the *omote shoin,* the front *shoin* of Tokushima Castle on the island of Shikoku. The castle complex, which today no longer exists, was built in 1587; its relatively large garden was probably completed by 1592. The garden received its present name – *Senshu-kaku,* "Pavilion of a Thousand Autumns" – in 1908. It combines a pond garden and a dry landscape garden based on the traditional Horai theme into a single harmonious whole. The two sections were designed to be enjoyed both on foot and from fixed vantage points in the now destroyed *shoin.*

Whereas the Muromachi era had given priority to the *kare-sansui* character of the garden, the Momoyama era sought to marry the "dry" and the "wet" so that the transition between the two appeared natural. The dry garden to the east of the *omote shoin* boasts probably Japan's longest bridge of natural stone; it is some 34 feet long with only one join. A second, slightly arched bridge of hewn stone, 18 feet long, was to prove another typical feature of the Momoyama garden. The pond section of the garden is characterized by standing stones and dry walls along the banks of the pond, which lies some four feet lower than the surrounding garden.

We shall next be examining three pond gardens

*Rock settings along the banks of the pond in
Senshu-kaku Park.*

The garden is seen framed by the right angles of
the wooden architecture. Sambo-in Temple,
Kyoto.

technique of garden design came to fullest fruition in
the gardens of the Edo era.[61]

Juraku-dai

Following the murder of Nobugana, power passed to
his most trusted vassal, Toyotomi Hideyoshi, the son of
a peasant. He succeeded in uniting the country under
his own hegemony by making peace with Ieyasu in
1558, subduing Kyushu in 1587 and conquering
northern Honshu in 1591. He also built a castle in
Kyoto on the site of the former Heian imperial palace.
He named it *Juraku-dai*, the "Mansion of Assembled
Pleasures". Nothing remains of this palatial residence,
however, nor of its splendid pond garden. Only *Hiun-
kaku*, the "Pavilion of the Flying Cloud" which probably formed part of Hideyoshi's private quarters, has
been preserved in Nishi Hogan-ji Temple in the south of
Kyoto, to where it was moved just before *Juraku-dai*
was dismantled. Hideyoshi subsequently retired to the
castle he had built in 1583 in nearby Osaka.

In 1594 he had a new castle built in Fushimi in the
Momoyama hills south-east of Kyoto. Its palace and
gardens were probably the most magnificent of the
Momoyama era, but they were not to endure: Fushimi
Castle was destroyed by earthquake and fire just
twenty years after Hideyoshi's death.

from the late Momoyama era which, according to
Mirei and Kanto Shigemori, are more subdued in their
expression and rockwork than their early Momoyama
predecessors. Thus the curves of their shorelines are
less dramatic, the rocks that follow them less obtrusive,
and the ponds themselves closer to ground level. Real
and dry waterfalls appear less sophisticated in their
composition. These gardens combine the qualities of
the "strolling" garden with the "picture" garden; their
leisurely-winding paths are designed to reveal a constant, fluid succession of new and scenic views. This

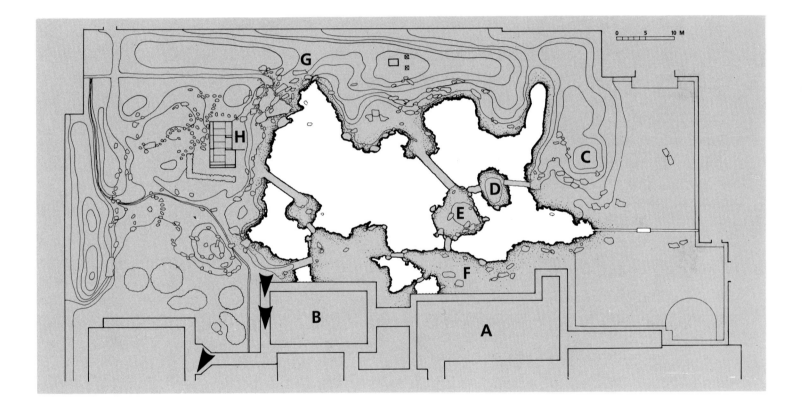

Sambo-in

There is still, however, one garden which survives to illustrate Hideyoshi's taste and influence. Although today part of *Sambo-in*, the "Three Treasure Temple", it remains closer in layout, size and atmosphere to a palace garden. In 1598 Hideyoshi decided to redesign an existing garden for one of his extravagant cherry-blossom parties. Work was not finally completed until after the event, by which time some seven hundred rocks and countless rare tree varieties – some from his previous *Juraku-dai* Palace – had been brought into the garden. It had become a common custom to transplant rocks famous for their size, shape, texture or colour from an older garden to a new one. Three hundred *kawaramono* were employed as labour. The garden itself covered an area of 650 square yards, and was conceived as a large-scale pond garden with turtle and crane islands and other motifs from the Horai myth. Despite the path meandering through its grounds and records of boating trips across its waters, there is no doubt that the garden is best viewed neither on foot nor by boat, but from the raised verandas of the *omote shoin* in the north-west and the *Junjokan* "Pure

123

*The right angles of the wooden architecture
appear to frame the garden beyond.*

*View from the Junjokan (Pure View Hall)
towards the waterfall in Sambo-in Pond
Garden.*

View Hall" at the centre of the complex. The rock composition located on the western peninsula represents the Horai Islands; a wooden bridge leads from here to the crane island, which is linked in turn to the turtle island by a short stone bridge. A bridge of earth connects the turtle island to the peninsula to the south. The alignment of these three bridges proved a characteristic feature of gardens of the Momoyama era: the first two, one long and one short, lie along one axis, while the third bridge, again long, branches off at a slight angle. Another recognizable feature of Momoyama gardens is the fact that the front garden separating the *shoin* from the pond is considerably narrower in depth than its counterparts in the Kamakura and Muromachi eras. The view from the *shoin* ends at a three-stepped waterfall at the foot of a high, forested hill in the south-east corner of the garden. Typical, too, of Momoyama pond gardens are tea arbours set within small and mysterious tea gardens.[62]

It is not known whether Hideyoshi actually saw the completion of the garden in which he had taken such personal interest, since he died very suddenly in 1598. The sheer number of its famous rocks and trees will ensure its survival as a memorial to the last, flamboyant attempt to revive the traditional pond-and-island garden. For despite its undeniably exquisite vistas and rock settings, the garden testifies first and foremost to the extravagance and exhibitionism both of Hideyoshi and the Momoyama era as a whole.

Nijo Castle

A similar stereotypical version of the pond garden comprises part of the *ni no maru*, the second keep of *Nijo* Castle just south of Hideyoshi's former Juraku-dai Palace. The pond in this garden, too, contains a large, central island representing Mount Horai and smaller crane and turtle islands. Nijo Castle was used by Tokugawa Ieyasu from 1601 onwards as a residence during his occasional visits to Kyoto. After his victory at Sekigahara in 1600, Ieyasu had become the undisputed ruler of a united Japan and the first of the Tokugawa shoguns. Just as Hideyoshi had entertained Emperor Goyozei at Juraku-dai in order to receive imperial sanction for the power he had so brutally obtained, so Iemitsu (1604 –1651), third Tokugawa shogun, decided to hold a reception for Emperor Gomizuno-o in autumn 1626. To this end he had *Nijo* Castle entirely remodelled between 1624 and 1626. His team of architects included Kobori Enshu, highly experienced in all the arts of the day and in the tea ceremony and garden-making in particular. A *gyoko goten* was built just south of the pond; this "August Hall for the Imperial Visit" was to be the emperor's temporary residence during his stay. Its components were moved to other sites after the visit had ended, and the present lawn laid in their place.

The impending imperial visit also led Iemitsu to turn many of the rock groups to face south towards the imperial residence. The garden is a classic example of a composition tailored to suit the rectangular buildings

The prolific array of large rocks employed in the pond garden of Nijo Castle complements the ostentatious architecture of the shogunal Grand Audience Hall.

framing three of its sides – the *gyoko goten* to the south, Iemitsu's *ohiroma*, or "Grand Audience Hall", to the east, and the magnificent *kuro-shoin* to the north. The garden's designers were thus faced with the task of creating a garden which appeared equally attractive from all three sides.

The garden's underlying theme is revealed in the large Horai island in the centre of its pond, with its strikingly monumental rock settings. A crane island lies to its north and a turtle island to its south. It seems appropriate that the garden of a shogun whose power was based chiefly on the military was also known as *Hachijin no niwa*, "Garden of Eight Camps": the layout of the garden and its peninsulas indeed mirror the strategic positions traditionally adopted by the seven army camps which surrounded the shogunal headquarters, here represented by the central Horai island. The present waterfall to the east is an addition of early Meiji times; the original waterfall, which could either carry real water or function as a dry composition as required, lay just to the south of it.

Since the floor of the pond is covered with pebbles, Shigemori suggests that the garden may have been originally designed both as a "dry" and a "wet" landscape. Particularly important in this respect is the bridge connecting the central Horai island to the mainland, since it reflects a fundamental reinterpretation of one of the most pervasive archetypes in Japanese garden art, namely the myth of Mount Horai.

This Isle of the Blest is no longer designed to appear far away and out of reach of ordinary mortals. It is now accessible on foot via a bridge. "Therefore", argues Shigemori, "from Momoyama times on gardens are designed by humans for humans. This signals a new trend in the creative arts."[63]

Whereas Hideyoshi's Sambo-in Temple Garden stood out for its collection of rocks of unusual shapes and textures, *Nijo* Castle Garden is memorable for the sheer quantity of rocks used. In this the garden undeniably complements the showy magnificence of the surrounding shogunal residence.

Genkyu-en

Genkyu-en, the "Park of the Mysterious Palace", in many ways foreshadows the large pond gardens of the Edo era. It was built between 1615 and 1624 at the north-eastern foot of *Hikone* Castle in Shiga Prefecture. Its scale is truly vast: it occupies an area of over five acres and contains two large and two small islands featuring outsized rock compositions. The western shore of the lake, behind which rises a steep hill, is the setting for various pavilions, some of them built on stilts over the water. Their rectangular wooden architecture frames the magnificent view out across the lake. To the north of the lake lies a hill called *Hosho-dai*, which translates literally as "the plateau from which the phoenix takes off". On the *Hosho-dai* stands a tea house commanding a view of the entire garden. The alignment of the three wooden bridges in the lake – two along the same axis and the third offset at a

Wooden bridge leading to the central island of Genkyu-en, the park at the foot of Hikone Castle.

Woodcut of the kare-sansui garden in Nishi-Hongan-ji temple, Kyoto, revealing the lavish use of huge rocks and exotic plants in Momoyama times (Source: "Miyako rinsen meisho zue", 1799).

slight angle – recalls those of *Sambo-in* and *Senshu-kaku*, and is typical of the Momoyama era.

The "beach island where the cranes sing", located in the northern part of the lake, features particularly large rocks on its southern shores, together with evergreen shrubs clipped into large designs. This and the smaller islands to the west undoubtedly compose one of the finest representations of the Horai myth to have survived from Momoyama times. In an era overshadowed by war and death, such "Isles of the Blest" became the concrete expression of prayers for a long and peaceful life.

The concept and layout of the garden reflect the dual roles of its creators, daimyo domain lords who were both *bushi,* warriors, and *bunjin*, men of learning. The extensive grounds and bold rock settings thus reflect the daimyo in their warrior capacity, while the hidden tea arbours around the lake, only accessible via mysterious stepping-stone paths, reveal them as learned connoisseurs of the tea ceremony.

Variational types of the Momoyama kare-sansui dry landscape garden

Kare-sansui, the new garden prototype accompanying a new type of architecture, was first "invented" in the Muromachi era. The *kare-sansui* gardens of the Momoyama era reveal the same preference for more and larger rocks already seen in the pond gardens of the same period.

Matsuo Shrine

One of the most important *kare-sansui* gardens of the Momoyama era is found within the precincts of Matsuo Shrine in Yokaichi in Shiga Prefecture. Mirei Shigemori rediscovered the garden in 1936; he dates it to between 1570 and 1590 and suggests it formed the southern front garden of a no longer existing *shoin*. The garden is exceptional for its shape, dictated by its site, whereby the view from the *shoin* is very deep and very narrow. The garden's designers were therefore obliged to place the turtle and crane islands one behind the other, rather than side by side as they were traditionally – simultaneously – viewed. The low-lying turtle island is now located directly in front of the *shoin*, while the crane island lies further back on an artificial hill. The largest standing rock on the crane island, well over five feet tall, represents the crane's wing. This garden is noticeably less abstract in character than its Muromachi predecessors, and is less derivative from Chinese landscape painting.[64]

Shinnyo-in

The dry garden of *Shinnyo-in*, the "Temple of Absolute Truth" in Kyoto, takes the shallow, oblong form typical of the Momoyama era. Typical, too, is its location on the south side of the *shoin*. It was allegedly created by Ashikaga Yoshiaki, who became Shogun in 1568 and was an ardent lover of gardens like his forebears. The garden was subsequently moved from its original

The dry waterfall in Kanji-in Temple Garden, Kyoto, after a woodcut in the first volume of the "Tsukiyama teizoden" of 1735.

Below:
Overall plan of the dry landscape garden in Hompo-ji Temple, Kyoto. (After a drawing in: Shigemori, M. and K., Takei, vol. 9, 1972)
A: Shoin; B: Storehouse ; C: Lotus pond;
D: Sun symbol composed of two carved stones;
E: Dry waterfall.

location and reconstructed in abridged form on the site we see today. The dry waterfall at its western end and the dry "stream" which passes in front of the *shoin* show it still indebted to the medieval gardens of the Muromachi era. New, however, is its use of double-layered symbolism, whereby the overlapping pattern of flat, bluish pebbles in the dry "river" resembles fishes' scales; these in turn symbolize the dynamic flow of water through the garden.

Kanji-in

The L-shaped garden in front of the *shoin* of *Kanji-in* in Kyoto was destroyed by fire in 1780. In our own century, the restored garden has suffered further with the construction of a hideous apartment block on its south side, an eyesore which spoils the view of the garden. It is nevertheless possible to identify from this garden two characteristic features of the gardens of the Momoyama era. The first is a bridge located above a two-stepped dry waterfall, with a rock triad behind symbolizing distant mountains. The rock settings on the two sides of the dry river are unusually well preserved. Similar dry waterfall compositions from the Muromachi era – *Tenryu-ji*, for example – all place their bridges *below* the waterfall. The waterfall also contains rocks whose purpose is to divide its imagined waters. In a second characteristic feature of Momoyama gardens, the middle of the garden is dominated by a sort of bay, which is visually concluded by a bridge of natural stone. In the centre of this bay lies a cylindrically-carved rock,

as used for bridge piers. It symbolizes a small island. Hewn stones would have been unthinkable in the dry gardens of the Muromachi era.

Hompo-ji

The juxtaposition of natural and geometrically-carved rocks within a single composition is a distinctive feature of Momoyama garden art. *Hompo-ji*, the "Temple of Original Law" in Kyoto, offers an even more startling example of such a combination. There is no written record of when or by whom the garden was created; Shigemori dates it, on stylistic grounds, to the 1570s or 1580s. The garden has the L-shape typical of the dry gardens of the times, whereby the longer arm of the L runs along the eastern side of the present *shoin* and the shorter arm follows it round to the south.

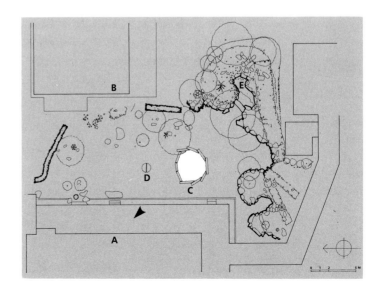

Flat, bluish pebbles are overlapped like the scales of a fish to symbolize the dynamic flow of water. Shinnyo-in Temple, Kyoto.

The dry landscape garden of Hompo-ji Temple, Kyoto, contains a "real" lotus pond. (After a woodcut in the "Miyako rinsen meisho zue")

The original garden must have extended further towards the north-east, but this area is today the site of a storehouse. In line with the typical format of Momoyama gardens, it has a dry waterfall with a bridge in front of it in the south-east. The dry "sea" in front of the *shoin* has lost the white sand and gravel that must once have covered it. If we may believe Ritoken Akisato, author of the *Miyako rinsen meisho zue*, the "Illustrated Manual of Celebrated Places in the Capital", the garden originally contained three artificial mountains in the form of a comma. Shigemori doubts their actual existence, however, believing it more likely that the sand of the dry sea in front of the *shoin* was raked into a whirlpool pattern suggestive of a comma. A highly unusual feature of the garden is its inclusion of carved stones; ten oblong, rectangular stones are interlinked to encircle a (real) lotus pond, while two semicircular stones laid together illustrate the ancient Chinese ideogram for "sun".

The temple belonged to the Buddhist Nichi-ren sect, and in Japanese the word *nichi-ren* means "sun-lotus". It thus symbolizes both shinto ideals of light and Buddhist ones of purity. The presence of this ideogram within the dry landscape garden is perhaps an indication that the garden was created not in the Momoyama era, but in the Edo period which followed.[65]

The setting of a "real" pond encircled by carved stones within a dry "sea" of white sand similarly displays an audacity not normally seen in the Momoyama era.

Nishi Hongan-ji

The best-preserved flat *kare-sansui* garden of the Momoyama era is *Kokei no niwa*, the "Tiger Glen Garden". It is now located within the precincts of *Hompo Nishi Hongan-ji* Temple in Kyoto, the headquarters of the Buddhist Jodo Shin sect founded by Shinran Shonin (1173–1263). It is thought that the garden was originally created for Hideyoshi's Fushimi Castle and was moved to its present site at a later date. In its current form the garden covers about a fifth of an acre. At its eastern end stands an artificial mountain with a *Shumisen* rock group. To the north of this lie a dry waterfall and crane and turtle islands in a central "sea" of sand. The garden is designed to be viewed like a painting from the veranda of the audience hall. The front garden separating the veranda from the dry pond is strikingly narrow; according to Shigemori, this was the indirect consequence of a fire in the seventeenth century

A bridge of a single slab of stone links a turtle and a crane island. Bridges hewn from a single stone were among the technical innovations of the Momoyama era. The sago palms are already wrapped in their winter coats.

*An island in a bay is here represented for
the first time by a rounded stone
such as those normally employed for
bridge-pier foundations.*

*The dry waterfall in Kanji-in as it appears
today. Above the waterfall, a bridge of natural
stone.*

View of the Konchi-in dry landscape garden after a woodcut from the "Miyako rinsen meisho zue" of 1799.

which destroyed the existing audience hall. In the version subsequently rebuilt, the front of the hall was extended some eighteen feet into the garden.

There are undeniable similarities between the layout of this dry landscape garden and that of Sambo-in temple garden. The siting of its waterfall and crane and turtle islands and its shoreline configurations all invite comparison. The alignment of its bridges is particularly noteworthy: here again, the first two bridges lie along the same virtually straight axis, while the third turns away at a sharp angle. Two of the bridges are made of hewn stone, one of natural stone; two are long and one is short.

What we see here is a dry landscape garden in the style of a pond garden. The *kare-sansui* garden of the Momoyama era thereby turns away from the abstract rock compositions of *Ryoan-ji* and the symbolic rock compositions of *Daisen-in*, its Muromachi predecessors, to return to more literal, iconic representations of crane and turtle islands, waterfalls and artificial mountains.[66]

If "less is more" was an appropriate description of the dry landscape gardens of the Muromachi era, the reverse is true of the Momoyama era. Its gardens overflow with rocks and exotic plants; austerity has been replaced by ostentation.

The combination of kare-sansui with o-karikomi

Momoyama garden-makers found unexpectedly new and powerful means of expression through the combination of the *kare-sansui* with *o-karikomi*, shrubs and bushes clipped into specific shapes. *Karikomi* was not in itself a novelty; it had formed a traditional aspect of Japanese gardens from their earliest beginnings. But it was only in the Momoyama era that it emerged as a primary feature of garden design.

The trend towards abstraction in Japanese garden art can be traced back to the earliest gardens of Nara and Heian times. Gardens were then composed of a few elements isolated from nature's infinite range of forms and surrounded by a man-made wall. The trend gained momentum in Kamakura and Muromachi times in the symbolic rock groups denoting *Shumi-sen*, the Buddhist mountain at the centre of the world, and turtle and crane islands, and in the white sand and pebbles indicating ponds and oceans. In the Momoyama and Edo eras, this trend took a new turn with the introduction of *o-karikomi*, the topiary art of clipping evergreen shrubs and bushes into shapes now only vaguely suggestive of such images as Mount Horai, treasure-laden ships and the storm-tossed sea. We owe the perfection of this art to just one man, Kobori Enshu (1579–1647).

As Mirei Shigemorei respectfully acknowledges, *o-karikomi* reached its climax and its end with the life – and death – of this great garden artist.[67]

A crane island (right) connected by a hewn stone slab bridge with the turtle island (left) amidst the sands of the Tiger Glen Garden which lies in front of the audience hall of Hompo Nishi-Hongan-ji Temple, Kyoto. It is thought that the garden was originally part of Hideyoshi's shogunal residence in Fushimi.

Bridges in both the pond and dry gardens of the Momoyama era were typically arranged in sets of three, two aligned and one at an angle.
A: Bridges of natural stone; B: Bridges of hewn stone; C: Bridges of wood; D: Bridges covered with earth.

Senshukaku Garden (dry)

Sambo-in Temple Garden (pond)

Nishihongan-ji Temple Garden (dry)

Genkyu-en Garden (pond)

North veranda of Shokin-tei Pavilion, Katsura Villa.

View of the o-karikomi in Daichi-ji Temple Garden.

The art of o-karikomi in Daichi-ji Temple Garden.
Topiary treasure ship in front of the shoin.

Raikyu-ji

History relates that Kobori Enshu designed the garden of *Raikyu-ji*, a Zen temple in Okayama Prefecture, about 1617. The garden combines a typical Zen-temple *kare-sansui* with a garden landscape whose central motifs are Mount Horai and crane and turtle islands. The most unusual and striking feature of the garden is its large-scale topiary representation of the waves of the ocean against the backdrop of a steep hill. The scene is entirely created with *tsubaki*, camellias in rows at the back, and *satsuki*, azaleas in curved lines at the front. Bearing in mind the practical difficulty of preserving such a "living sculpture" in its original form

over the centuries, this illustration of the Horai motif remains one of the most remarkable of its kind. *O-karikomi* has here become a design tool in its own right.

Directly in front of the *shoin* lies a crane island composed of clipped azaleas and an unusually beautiful group of some twenty rocks. When viewed from the *shoin*, these rocks appear to compose a *Shumi-sen* group. When viewed from the *hondo*, the main hall in the north, however, they appear as a triadic composition set against the "borrowed" background of Mount Atago in the distance.

The turtle island in the south of the garden has unfortunately been destroyed, and its original form is unknown. Shigemori believes that the small stream and pond below the clipped bushes in the south of the garden are additions of the late Edo or Meiji era. Under the wide eaves of the *hondo* lies a rectangular field strewn with pebbles. It is crossed by carefully-placed stepping-stones, and contains a water basin similar to those in the temples of Konchi-in and Koho-an in Kyoto. Both of these temples are known to have been designed by Kobori Enshu.

Daichi-ji

Daichi-ji, the "Temple of the Great Pond", is located in Minakuchi in Shiga Prefecture. The garden immediately east of its *shoin* contains an *o-karikomi* of clipped azaleas, which is ascribed to Kobori Enshu or one of his successors. It is said to represent an enormous treasure ship carrying the "seven gods of good luck" of Chinese mythology. In another interpretation, it is seen as

Garden of Konchi-in, a sub-temple of Nanzen-ji Temple, Kyoto. The head of the turtle island is represented in the dynamic sweep of a diagonal rock.

a large crane island counterbalanced by a small turtle island lying directly beneath the eaves of the *shoin*. The turtle's body is composed of a single clipped bush, with a single stone for its head. The composition as a whole appears somewhat softer in its contours than *Raikyu-ji*, perhaps because its rock components play a quieter role. Noteworthy, too, are the garden behind the tea house and the *karikomi* beneath a venerable pine tree outside the entrance to the temple.

Konchi-in

Konchi-in is a sub-temple within the Zen monastery of *Nanzen-ji* at the foot of the mountains east of Kyoto.

The abbot's quarters, accompanying tea house and Toshogu shrine were designed by Kobori Enshu on behalf of an influential Zen priest called Suden; they were subsequently executed in 1628 under Kobori Enshu's personal supervision. The work itself was carried out by now highly-respected *kawaramono*, among them a certain Kentei, the last "riverside worker" to be mentioned in official records. He had also worked on Sambo-in and other famous Momoyama gardens. The garden attached to the south side of the *hojo*, also designed by Kobori Enshu, was completed by 1632.

The area of sand immediately in front of the *hojo* is raked into the shape of a boat. To the east and west lie, respectively, a turtle and a crane island, equidistant from the central axis of the abbot's quarters. Between these two islands, and directly aligned with the central axis, there lies a large, flat *reihaiseki*, a worshipping stone within a field of bluish pebbles. This *reihaiseki* relates to the Toshogu shrine, whose roof can just be discerned to the west of it. The shrine itself was dedicated to the spirit of Shogun Ieyasu.

The view southwards ends in an *o-karikomi*, which conceals the sharp fall of the land. The topiary forms created here are different, however, to those encountered in the two abovementioned gardens. Apart from perhaps representing the waves in whose midst the Isles of the Blest are sited, they appear to have no symbolic character and instead serve purely decorative purposes.

Senshu-kaku Pond Garden, sited below
Tokushima Castle, displays surely the most
dramatic rock grouping of the Momoyama era.

The *naka-roji*, the middle garden which is reached via the *naka-kuguri*, is more accurately the inner tea garden serving *zangetsu-tei*, the "Pavilion of the Waning Moon". This Shoin-style tea house has its own *tobi-ishi* and *tsukubai*. The *naka-kuguri* is the only means of entrance to the pavilion, which was built by Rikyu's adopted son and modelled on Rikyu's own *shoin* quarters in Hideyoshi's Juraku-dai palace. "In its nobility of concept and design", writes Teiji Itoh, it is "fully qualified to present itself as a pioneer structure in the Sukiya style."[72] We shall be discussing this new style of Japanese architecture in the next chapter. Meanwhile, the Zangetsu-tei that we see today is in fact a reconstruction from 1913.

Following the stepping-stones through the *naka-roji*, the middle garden, we pass a square well (H), artistically designed with a lid cover and pulley system. Most city dwellers obtained their water from private wells such as this one, and its importance for the tea ceremony is underlined by its central location within the garden. Reaching the end of the middle garden, we pass through a simple gate, the *baiken-mon* or "plum-viewing gate" (I), and enter the *uchi-roji* inner tea garden. The components of this inner *roji* are the same as those of the outer garden. The more barriers that have to be passed on the way to the *so-an*, the tea arbour, the more sacred the site appears.

Immediately after the *baiken-mon* to the right is the *uchi-koshikake*, the inner waiting booth with its long, covered bench seat (J). It offers guests a place to relax during the full tea ceremony, which lasts some four

hours. The ceremony is divided into two parts: a light meal is served in the first half, and in the second half two sorts of tea, first strong and then weak. Guests usually retreat to the *uchi-koshikake* in the short interval between the two.

Near the *uchi-koshikake* lies a second small "decorative toilet", the *suna setchin* or *kazari setchin* (K). It is designed for our aesthetic appreciation rather than practical use. Stepping-stones lead us on past a stone lantern (L) and a washing basin (M) towards the entrance of our goal, *fushin-an* tea arbour.

Since tea ceremonies were held at night as well as during the day, lanterns were required to light the path

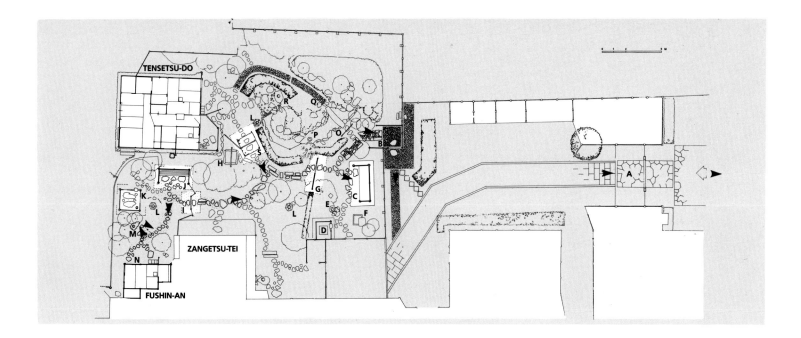

across the *roji*. These lanterns were usually placed near gates, at unexpected bends in the path or near washing basins. The stone lanterns, *ishi-doro*, introduced by the tea masters of the sixteenth century had previously been used in temples and shrines. The stone lantern in the inner *roji* of *fushin-an* is based on the style of those lining the approach to the Kasuga shrine in Nara.

Before entering the tea arbour, the guest washes his hands and rinses his mouth in a second *tsukubai* stone basin (M). This physical act has a symbolic importance: the guest is cleansed of any worldly defilement and cares before proceeding to the tea ceremony. Similar stone basins for symbolic washing rituals are found in Shinto shrines and Buddhist temples from the thirteenth century onwards. In Japanese *roji* they are usually found near the entrance to the tea house.

Tsukubai literally means "a place where one has to bend down". It is always sunk lower than the level of the garden and, as its name suggests, requires the guest to squat down to reach it – an important act of humility. The depression in which the *tsukubai* lay became known as the "sea". The largest stone in the *tsukubai* rock group is called *chozubachi*, "hand water basin". In tea gardens built in Sen no Rikyu's *wabi* style, *chozubachi* are usually very simple, natural rocks with a hollowed centre. A bamboo ladle to scoop out the water is usually provided on top of the stone. To the right and left of the *chozubachi* lie two flat stones. During tea ceremonies, a bucket of hot water is placed on one and a lantern on the other. The guest himself stands on a third stone, placed directly before the

chozubachi. Like the stones used for the *tobi-ishi* and around the stone lanterns, the rocks employed in the *tsukubai* were originally selected on the basis of predominantly functional criteria. With time, however, they attracted increasing aesthetic interest. As form became more important than function, so *tsukubai* can today also be seen in gardens unconnected with the tea ceremony.

It is not far from the *tsukubai* to the Fushin-an tea arbour itself. The entrance lies through another "crawl-through gate", the *nijiri-guchi* (N). Like the *naka-kuguri* encountered earlier, it contains a square door measuring about 2 x 2 feet. The guest is once again made highly conscious of his body as he crawls through the small hole, just as he is once again reminded of the humility with which he should enter the inner sactum. All social rank is temporarily suspended in the tea house and garden for the duration of the tea ceremony. Looking up as you emerge through the gate into the tea arbour, you are confronted by a *tokonoma*, a decorative alcove. This usually contains a picture scroll and a flower arrangement, specially selected by the host for the occasion.

The *nijiri-guchi* is thought to have been introduced by Sen no Rikyu, who may have known of similar small "crawl-through" entrances from the storehouses and farm buildings of Korea. Its psychological effect upon the guest is dialectical: the very small tea arbour, which measures just three tatami in size (6 square yards), feels much bigger when you have just squeezed through an even tinier door. Walking fully-erect into the same

View from Shokin-tei, the Pine Lute pavilion, towards a garden scene representing Amanohashidate, the "Bridge of Heaven". This long, pine-covered sand bar is one of the three famous natural sights in Japan's Tango province. The garden here seems to extend right into the tea room itself.

Path of natural stones leading to the outer
waiting booth of Shokin-tei tea arbour, which
lies out of sight further down the path.

Aesthetic ideals of the Momoyama era and their influence on garden design

Wabi – restraint and poverty

That the Muromachi dry landscape garden and the Momoyama rustic tea garden should be so different comes as something of a surprise. They are, after all, both products of Zen, the former inspired by Zen aesthetics and the latter by the dictum that "Zen and tea have the same taste". But the tea garden is neither dry nor austere like the *kare-sansui*, nor does it focus upon a dramatic rock composition. Instead it is damp and often carpeted with moss. Its stepping-stones and paths may even be constantly sprinkled with water. It avoids brightly-coloured flowers which could distract the guest's attention and usually favours quieter evergreens, particularly those with shiny foliage. The only touch of colour might be a small-leafed maple or plum tree blossoming in early spring. The Momoyama attitude towards nature, and towards the creation of man-made nature, has now reached such a level of sophistication that the tea garden is designed to appear "artless", even "ordinary". This is the new aesthetic ideal of *wabi*, implying a taste for the ordinary, the simple, the common, the modest, the rustic.

The *wabi-cha* tea ritual conceived by Sen no Rikyu is based upon an aesthetic of restraint in every respect: the setting for the tea ceremony is kept as small as possible, colours are subdued and decorative utensils reduced to a minimum. It is a world of withdrawal from earthly pomp. It often appears close to the medieval concept of *sabi*, the love for the withered, the patina of age. But the aesthetic of *wabi* in fact goes far deeper.

Sen no Rikyu's attitude towards garden design is perhaps best illustrated in the following historical anecdote. Entering a tea garden one fine morning, he found the ground littered with leaves shed by a mountain tree planted in the garden. He was enchanted by this natural scene. When he returned a few hours later for the tea ceremony, however, he found his host had

160

View from Shokin-tei Pine Lute pavilion
across the central pond to the old shoin of
Katsura Villa, Kyoto.
(see pp. 26, 166–167)

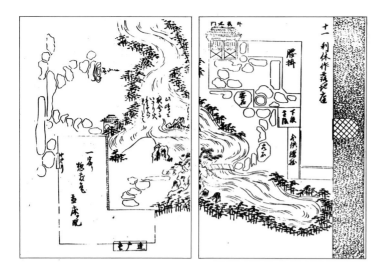

swept up all the leaves. This did not please him at all, and he is reported to have shaken a tree gently until a few leaves had again fallen to the ground. He then gave instructions that the garden should not be swept immediately before the tea ceremony, but rather a few hours in advance, to allow at least a few leaves to fall in the interim. At the same time as insisting upon utter cleanliness, Sen no Rikyu thus also wanted the tea garden to look natural. The garden was to imitate the processes of nature. Sen no Rikyu illustrated predominantly rural themes in his garden designs, which are frequently dominated by a simple rustic cottage with a thatched roof. Nor should it be forgotten that these isolated mountain retreats are located right in the heart of the city.

Suki – personal preference and taste

Japanese garden scholar Seidai Tanaka, in his book on the Japanese garden, takes as his main theme the rupture between Sen no Rikyu and his pupil, Furuta Oribe, inspired above all by their different attitudes to the tea garden. According to Tanaka, Oribe – unlike Sen no Rikyu – was uninterested in the mere imitation of nature's mode of operation. He would sweep away any leaves that fell in his garden and spread the ground evenly with pine needles instead. These he would scatter not just beneath trees of both coniferous and deciduous species, but also around the edges of stepping-stones. This human interference with nature is similarly reflected in his mixing of natural and dressed

stones in pathways, and in his carpeting of the outer *roji* with bluish pebbles from the ocean and of the inner *roji* with pine needles. These two artificial surfaces were then crossed by stepping-stones.[74]

The "rupture" which Tanaka argues took place between Rikyu and Oribe is of vital significance for the history of the Japanese garden. For Oribe imitates nature neither in its outer form (as in the Nara and Heian eras), nor in its inner essence (Kamakura and Muromachi eras), nor even in its mode of operation (Sen no Rikyu). Indeed, he does not imitate nature at all. He begins instead to create a new, second nature, by sanctifying the use of geometric forms such as rectangular stones, and by allowing his personal preferences and artistic tastes to govern the overall design of his gardens. Thus pine needles fall under deciduous trees, as man's creative will is set against that of nature.

Sakui – creativity and originality

The new aesthetic ideals developed by the tea masters were ultimately dependent upon the originality of the individual designer. Emphasis was now placed upon *sakui*, personal creativity, rather than upon the imitation of patterns of nature or historical models. One aspect of this new creativity lay in the reinterpretation of traditional values and the imaginative redeployment of existing objects. Examples here include the stone lanterns and water basins encountered earlier; these had long been in use in shrines and temples, but when introduced into the tea garden assumed an entirely new significance.

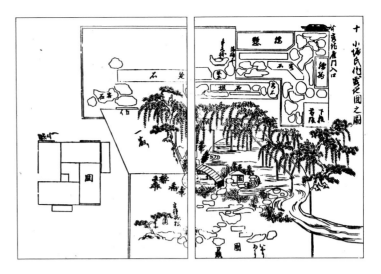

Shokoku chaniwa meiseki zue: an illustrated manual of famous tea gardens

The *Shokoku chaniwa meiseki zue* – an "Illustrated Manual of Famous Remnants of Tea Gardens of Various Countries" – originally formed part of the *Kokin chado zenshu,* a compendium of writings on the ritual and setting of the tea ceremony which was first published in 1694. The fifth volume of the *Kokin chado zenshu* was devoted specifically to the tea garden, and rapidly sold out. It was therefore republished separately in two volumes under the title *Shokoku chaniwa meiseki zue.* Its contents are not, however, the secret, orally-transmitted teachings of earlier treatises on garden-making. Three double-page illustrations from the *Shokoku* are reproduced above. They supposedly show gardens designed by the three of the most influential early tea masters: Sen no Rikyu, Furuta Oribe and Kobori Enshu.

The graphic technique employed in these illustrations reveals a new approach to the portrayal of gardens, combining and superimposing both horizontal and vertical planes. Thus certain features, such as buildings and paths, are seen in plan, while others, such as trees, rocks, mountains, lanterns and bridges, are shown in elevation. All three illustrations show an outer and inner *roji* separated by a stream, which is crossed by a bridge. Each of these three gardens represents a passageway to the ultimate goal of the tea arbour. The drawings employ what might be termed a primitive system of sequential notation to record the events along these paths.

In terms of detail, Sen no Rikyu's garden is the simplest of the three, employing solely natural elements. Oribe's garden is more elaborate, more consciously a garden; it features paths of dressed stones, stone lanterns and a water basin. Kobori Enshu, master of the topiary landscape, goes even further than Oribe; even the plants in his garden are physically subject to the designer's will.

These drawings also reflect the importance to the designer of the close interplay of buildings and gardens. This found its most elegant solution in the architecture of the Sukiya style, and its juxtapositioning, overlapping and balancing of the right angle and natural form. Why else should rectangular paving-stones suddenly appear along the path, if not to enhance, by way of contrast, the beauty of the indefinable forms of nature?

Shigure-tei, the "Autumn Shower Pavilion", is linked via an open pergola to Kasa-tei Pavilion in the background.

Kasa-tei, the "Umbrella Pavilion". Both pavilions now form part of Kodai-ji Temple in Kyoto.

Square stepping-stones stray across the small, pebble cobbles of a zigzagging path beneath the eaves of Onrin-do, a small memorial temple in Katsura Villa.

Shirakawa Bridge, as seen from Shokin-tei Pavilion. In typical Momoyama style the bridge consists of a single hewn stone.

View of the pebble peninsula representing Amanohashidate, one of Japan's three most famous natural sights. A classic example of the technique of shukkei, the small-scale reproduction of real objects, in the eastern section of Katsura Villa Pond Garden.

名所

Famous views from literature and reality

Gardens as substitutes for travel

The gardens of the Edo era are largely stereotypical imitations of the pond-and-island and dry landscape gardens of earlier times. Both, however, make new use of *shakkei*, the technique of incorporating more distant elements of the surrounding landscape into the garden design. This same period also sees the development of a new garden prototype, the garden for strolling, in which a prespecified circuit takes the visitor past a succession of *meisho*, or "famous sights". These may be actual geographical features, faithfully recreated on a smaller scale or alluded to by other means, or they may be imaginary places sung about in poetry. This fourth prototype offers a fresh synthesis of elements from each of its three predecessors. The gardens were designed by professional garden artists, *niwa-shi*, and were usually commissioned by rich daimyo princes. The garden for strolling is a secularized garden which aims at a selective realistic imitation of the outer forms of nature. As such it belongs to the tradition of the gardens of the Heian period. At the same time, however, its considerably grander scale reflects the new tastes of the Edo era.

From the Edo to the Meiji era

The Tokugawa shoguns, whose authority was derived
– initially, at least – from the imperial court, proved ex-
tremely successful politicians. Over the next two and a
half centuries they were to maintain peaceful rule and
secure the continuing hegemony of their family.

Political system and class society

During this period the Tokugawa shoguns adopted a
policy of isolationism towards the outside world. They
refused both trade and cultural exchanges with foreign
countries. Internally, they sought to maintain the status
quo by rigidly stratifying Japanese society into social
classes between which no movement was possible,
using neo-Confucian ethics to underpin their system.
At the top of the social pecking order were the shoguns and their families, followed by their daimyo vassals and the samurai below them. Last of all came
farmers, artisans and merchants. Each class of society
generated its own culture and aesthetic ideals.

Social stability and internal peace were preserved in
part by legislative means. The *Sankin kotai* "law of alternate attendance" was passed in two parts in 1635
and 1642. Daimyo lords were thereby obliged to spend
one half of the year in the capital, Edo. Even during the
six months spent back in their own domains they were
required to leave their families in Edo, effectively providing the Tokugawas with hostages in the event of
political intrigue. It was a system of control which

weakened the daimyo nobles both politically and fi-
nancially: most of their resources now were spent on
their half-yearly journeys to and from Edo and on the
maintenance of one or several additional residences in
the capital.

A by-product of this system of enforced migration
was the development of an efficient road network
across the country. Edo, too, profited from its enriched
mixture of peoples and ideas from all over Japan. This
system of alternate attendance proved a success in so
far as it indeed prevented any revolt by daimyo vassals.
But the drain it placed on daimyo resources was ultimately to bring about the collapse of the entire feudal
economy.

The rise of a merchant culture

In an irony of history, the urban merchants who ranked
lowest in Edo society slowly grew to enjoy the greatest
wealth and prosperity. This in turn led to an outburst of
creative activity in the arts, sponsored and encouraged
by a newly-affluent bougeoisie. The warrior and farmer
classes, on the other hand, whose income was drawn
entirely from agriculture, found themselves growing
increasingly poorer.

The period from the late seventeenth to the early
eighteenth century is known as the Genroku epoch.
During this time, both cultural and economic activity
was centred around Osaka and, to a lesser degree,
Kyoto. Edo was both too young and, at the same time,
out of line with the new spirit of the age. It remained

dominated by the samurai ethic of *Bushido*, the "Way of the Warrior" clearly misplaced in a period of extended peace. Whereas samurai culture continued to revolve around the traditional arts of Noh theatre, the tea ceremony and flower arranging, the rising class of urban merchants focussed upon the new, rather more plebeian art forms of Kabuki theatre and Bunraku puppet plays. Literature and theatre now took their themes from the *ukiyo*, the "floating world", found in the decadent, frivolous pleasure districts of towns and cities. To this period, too, belong the travel writings of Basho and the art of the haiku, a form of poetry employing only seventeen syllables. A further significant development was the shift in interest away from the individual painting, the unique work of art, towards the reproducible medium of the woodcut print. These prints were initially only available in black and white; by the middle of the eighteenth century, however, they were appearing in multiple colours and halftones. Their subjects reflect the preoccupations of the merchant classes: Kabuki actors and beautiful prostitutes are recurring themes of these *ukiyo-e*, "pictures of the floating world".

The period from the late eighteenth to the early nineteenth century is called the Bunka-Bunsai epoch. In these late Tokugawa times, the centre of creative activity and cultural life in general gradually shifted away from Osaka and Kyoto to Edo, present-day Tokyo. Although the epoch brought no great innovations in literature or theatre, it saw a flowering of painting with the adoption of elements of Chinese

bunjin, an academic style of painting characterized by soft colours and delicate brushwork. Nagasaki, in the south of Japan, was the only port open to Chinese *bunjin* artists during the Edo era. The first Portuguese *namban*, or "southern barbarians", also settled here, along with a few Dutch merchants.

The important developments which appeared in the techniques and themes of the *ukiyo-e* are linked above all with the names of woodcut artists Katsushika Hokusai (1760–1849) and Ando Hiroshige (1797–1858). Both had learnt new techniques from the Western world which they introduced into their Japanese art, while their colourful prints in turn had great influence on Western painting. Each in his own way adapted block printing to landscape subjects, setting seasonal moods and various human activities against a backdrop of famous natural sights. The Japanese landscape will be forever immortalized in series such as Hokusai's "36 Views of Mount Fuji" and Hiroshige's "53 Stations along the Tokaido".

Intellectual trends and counter-trends

The orthodox Confucian ethic supported by the Tokugawa shoguns clearly suited their political interests. It demanded unquestioning acceptance of existing class relationships and thus provided the ideological foundation for a rigid social hierarchy. Inevitably, however, there arose other schools of thought opposed to Tokugawa neo-Confucianism. The *Kogaku-ha* "School of Ancient Learning", for example, questioned the hereditary system of power tranference within the Tokugawa family, and advocated a return to the original tenets of Confucius, who had made the right to rule dependent upon intellectual and scholarly merit. The *Bushido*, the samurai ethical code, was also formulated by thinkers of the *Kogaku-ha* school. A second school of thought existing during the eighteenth and nineteenth centuries rejected the Chinese ethic outright. *Kokugaku-ha*, the "School of National Learning", denounced neo-Confucianism as a foreign body of thought and behaviour and devoted itself to a study of the origins of the Japanese language and literature in the search for the nation's innermost soul. With their acceptance of the Shinto pantheon and the divine lineage of the Emperor, they paved the way towards the restoration of imperial rule and the nationalism of Meiji times. During the Meiji era, previously half-Confucian, half-Shinto Japan came to be entirely dominated by Shintoism.

A third school of heterodox thought, *Rangaku-ha*, or "School of Dutch Studies", was the product of Dutch influence. In the eighteenth century Holland was the only European country still permitted to trade with Japan from a small base in Nagasaki. The Dutch represented a second wave of Western influence; fear of foreign ideas, in particular Christianity, had led to the abrupt termination of a first wave of European infiltration during the civil wars of the Momoyama era. The interests of the *Rangaku-ha* school were technical and practical rather than philosophical or ideological, and its products included treatises on medicine, cartography and the techniques of perspective drawing.

With the decline of Tokugawa supremacy, it became increasingly clear that the key problems facing Japanese modernization were "the need for a combination of Eastern morals and Western technology" and the

question of "how to retain the socially binding ethics of traditional behavior while at the same time resolutely acquiring the material benefits of the Western scientific and industrial revolution"[75].

Stereotypical forms of the Edo pond garden

Many pond gardens were created during Edo times, the most beautiful and expressive of them in the early part of the era. Many of them form part of Buddhist temple complexes, where they are often attached to the *shoin* of the abbot's quarters. Although laid out as gardens for strolling, they are best appreciated from fixed vantage points, such as from inside the *shoin*, where they can be viewed as three-dimensional pic-

tures framed by the rectangular lines of the building. What is new, however, is that many of them are built on existing natural slopes, obviating the need to build artificial hills specially for the garden. The close proximity of their ponds to a *shoin* or Buddha Hall had its practical reasons, too: these predominantly wooden structures were frequently swept by fire. The ponds thus functioned as a reservoir, supplying water with which to fight the flames. We shall be examining four of the most important pond gardens below.

Emman-in

The garden of *Emman-in*, once part of Enjo-ji Temple in Otsu, is attached to the south of a Shinden-style hall which was donated to the temple in 1647 by Emperor Meisho. Shigemori dates the garden to around this same period. Its layout resembles that of Hideyoshi's *Sambo-in* garden from the Momoyama era. Its elongated, east-west oriented pond contains a turtle and a crane island. In the style of the times, a large rock on the eastern shore of the pond symbolizes Mount Horai. The rock arrangements along the nearby banks number among the most beautiful in the garden. The ground rises steeply behind the pond, allowing the designer to create a proper mountain path. A stream flows into the pond from the south-west, behind which, higher up the hillside, there lies a dry waterfall. Emman-in as a whole is a classic example of a garden attached to the living quarters within a temple complex.

173

Above:
Layout of the elongated, east-west oriented pond garden on the south side of the shinden in Emman-in Temple, Otsu.

Below:
Layout of the narrow pond garden in Ojogo-kuraku-in, the Temple of Rebirth in Paradise, a sub-temple of Sanzen-in in Ohara, north of Kyoto.

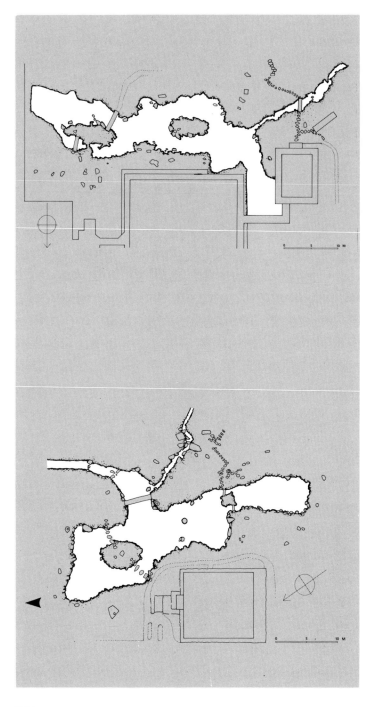

Sanzen-in

Sanzen-in Temple, belonging to the Tedai sect of Buddhism, lies to the north of Kyoto. The pond garden attached to one of its sub-temples – *Ojogokuraku-in*, the "Temple of Rebirth in Paradise" – may have been modelled on *Emman-in*. Built only a little later, between 1648 and 1654, it also makes use of an existing slope and features a long and narrow pond with turtle and crane islands. Its shoreline is somewhat more undulating than that of its predecessor. A stream flows into the pond from the hill in the east.

Unlike *Emman-in*, however, this garden is not attached to a *shoin* from whose veranda it would be viewed. This leads Shigemori to suggest it was designed from the very start with a different aim in mind, namely to be a water reservoir in the event of a fire in the main hall, which contained a precious statue of Amida Buddha. This practical necessity is then transformed into garden art. A large number of tall Japanese cedars and maple trees shade an immaculately-kept expanse of moss to the north of the pond.[76]

Chishaku-in

Chishaku-in Temple in south-east Kyoto belongs to the Buddhist Shingon sect and was probably built in 1674. Its pond garden lies alongside the abbot's quarters and the main temple hall on a north-south axis and, like the other pond gardens of its time, skilfully integrates a steep hillside to the east into its overall design.

The garden of Chishaku-in Temple, Kyoto, where
a steep natural slope is incorporated into the
garden architecture.

The section of the garden around the north side of the
shoin is an afterthought of late Edo or Meiji origin;
its composition appears considerably weaker. Although
a path invites a stroll across the hillside, the garden still
presents its most captivating view from the *shoin* and
its veranda. The location of the pond directly beneath
the *shoin* is out of keeping with the garden architecture of the day; Shigemori therefore surmises that the
present garden dates from the period after the temple
fire of 1682. The composition on the eastern hillside
focuses upon a dry waterfall bridged by a single hewn
stone. Rock settings of dry waterfalls on steep hillsides

were to prove something of a typical feature of Edo
pond gardens. In front of the dry waterfall, in the
pond, lies an exquisitely-shaped rock island. The carv-
ing of a through into the main falling water stone and
the running of actual water, as seen in the photo on
page 219, is of recent origin. Three bluish, flat natural
stones form a bridge to the hillside. This bridge, decidedly Muromachi or Momoyama in style, is perhaps the
sole survivor of an earlier garden on the same site.[77]

Joju-in

Joju-in is a pond garden on the north side of the *hojo*,
the abbot's quarters, within the famous Kiyomizu Temple in the hills south-east of Kyoto. The garden in its
present form probably dates from the Genroku epoch
(1688–1703). The pond still features turtle and crane
islands; the larger turtle island is linked to the mainland
by two bridges, one of natural stone and the other of
wood covered with a layer of earth. The large rock
which stands at the centre of the turtle island is similar
in shape to the traditional headwear formerly worn by
nobles and priests, from whence it derives its name,
eboshi. The Edo era showed a growing fondness for
such curiosities. They delighted in strangely-shaped
rocks, stone lanterns and water basins. The smaller
crane island lies in the south-eastern part of the pond.

The hill to the east is covered with clipped azalea
bushes which gradually merge into the natural landscape towards the boundaries of the garden. At the
same time, a stone lantern placed in a small clearing

Pond garden of Joju-in temple, Kyoto, with a furisode water basin which can be used directly from the veranda.

draws the eye out towards the distant mountains in the north. The viewer is thereby doubly tricked: the merging of clipped and unclipped vegetation and the drawing of the distant mountains into the visual field make the garden appear much bigger than it actually is, namely a mere 710 square yards. A second stone lantern on the island in the pond and a horizontally-clipped hedge along the northern edge of the garden are further devices by which the far mountains are "borrowed" for the overall composition. The stone lantern has clearly long since lost its original function as a source of illumination in temples and shrines and subsequently along the winding paths of *roji* tea gardens. It now serves to create an illusion of depth. Another fashionable element of Edo gardens is found immediately in front of the veranda, in the form of the *furisode*, a stone basin shaped like the long sleeve of a kimono. The *furisode* too has lost its original function as a place of purification.

Stereotypical forms of the Edo dry landscape garden

The early Edo era saw a rich renaissance of the dry landscape garden. Shigemori discusses no less than forty-four such gardens from this period in his book on the *kare-sansui*. But just as the pond gardens discussed above are merely small-scale replicas of earlier Heian and Muromachi prototypes, so the dry landscape gardens of the Edo era are little more than stereotypical imitations of their Muromachi forebears. The period

produces nothing to compare with either the strict rectangular framework and highly abstract composition of a *Ryoan-ji*, nor the free layout and naturalistic scenery of a *Taizo-in*. Naturally we should not forget that even these owed much to Chinese monochrome landscape painting. We will be discussing below two of the finest *kare-sansui* gardens of the Edo era, the first illustrating the tradition of "natural scenery" and the second the tradition of "abstract composition" in the dry landscape garden.

Manshu-in

Manshu-in lies in the foothills north-east of Kyoto. Created in 1656, the garden is attached to the large and small *shoin*. Both the overall design and individual details of the garden suggest that this is a pond garden laid out in dry form. It is best viewed from the small *shoin*, from where it reveals all the traditional attributes of a dry landscape garden representing natural scenery. These include an artificial mountain with a rock group symbolizing Mount Horai on the left, a bridge of natural stone which crosses a dry stream, a peninsula which is linked via a second bridge of stone slabs to a crane island in the far west, a triadic rock composition and a stone lantern on the crane island itself, and in front a turtle island floating in a "sea" of white sand. A series of *tobi-ishi* (stepping-stones) leads across the narrow strip of garden between the east wall of the small *shoin* and the steeply-rising hillside, ending at a small rustic tea arbour attached to the *shoin*.

A dry landscape garden in the "natural scenery" tradition: Manshu-in Temple Garden, seen from the veranda of the large shoin. In the foreground, the turtle island.

Nanzen-ji

Nanzen-ji, at the foot of the hills east of Kyoto, is a Zen temple of the Rinzai sect. The south garden in front of the *hojo* belongs to the *Ryoan-ji* tradition of Zen temple gardens. Like almost all the dry gardens of the Genroku epoch (1688–1703), however, and despite being only slightly smaller in size (510 square yards compared to *Ryoan-ji*'s 645), *Nanzen-ji* differs significantly from its Muromachi predecessor both in its overall composition and its rock settings. In *Ryoan-ji* and *Shinju-an*, for example, the entire garden was given over to sets of

rocks combined into abstract compositions. In *Nanzen-ji*, on the other hand, the garden surface is largely empty, covered simply with finely-raked white sand. Just one corner is reserved for rocks and plants, exhibited for their size and natural form rather than grouped to form an abstract composition. We see here a trend away from abstraction and symbolism and towards a more naturalistic handling of garden elements. These gardens are no longer designed for contemplation, but rather for show purposes.

Shakkei: "borrowed" scenery in pond and dry landscape gardens of the Edo era

Both the pond gardens and the dry landscape gardens of the Edo era gain a new dimension through the skilful use of *shakkei*, the technique of borrowing distant scenery for their own compositional purposes.

Teiji Itoh traces the origins of the term *shakkei* in his book "Space and Illusion in the Japanese Garden". It first appeared in the seventeenth century in Chinese writings on garden art, and was adopted by the Japanese some time during the nineteenth century. By that point, however, the actual technique of *shakkei* had long been employed in Japanese garden design. The earliest and best-known example is Tenryu-ji Temple Garden of Kamakura times, which draws Mount Arashiyama into its composition.

The orginal Japanese term for the technique of *shakkei* was *ikedori*, which means "to capture alive". This term makes it clear that *shakkei* is more than just a

The dry landscape garden of Entsu-ji temple, Kyoto, with the borrowed silhouette of Mount Hiei.

view of a section of the distant landscape. It is the art of "capturing alive" both natural features, such as mountains, hills and plains, and man-made structures, such as temple gates and pagodas. The devices by which such background features were framed and drawn into the garden fall into four distinct compositional planes receding from the foreground to the far background. While the foreground itself plays a minor role, the middle ground is the site of carefully-positioned objects serving to link foreground and background. The trees and hedges of the background in turn create the frame through which to view the

fourth and final plane containing the distant scenery. Three examples may serve to illustrate the popularity of the *shakkei* technique, which was employed in all types of Edo garden except the tea garden.

Entsu-ji temple in Kyoto contains probably the most famous *shakkei* garden in Japan. This flat, dry landscape garden to the east of the main hall measures 790 square yards and is generally believed to date from around 1678. Its rectangular surface is entirely carpeted with moss and features a number of – chiefly horizontal – rock arrangements. The garden is bordered to the east, south and north by a hedge about four feet high. Viewed from the veranda of the main hall, the garden captures the upper part of Mount Hiei, Kyoto's highest peak lying some four miles away to the north-east of the city. The mountain is framed by tall-trunked Japanese cedars and white cypresses rising just beyond the garden hedge. The foliage of the trees at the top and the horizontals of the bamboo grove and clipped hedge at the bottom complete the sides of this "window" onto distant nature. There was originally a large horizontal boulder on the moss directly beneath Mount Hiei, which would have reinforced the link between background and foreground. To witness the first autumn moon rising behind Mount Hiei from the veranda must be a breathtaking sight indeed.

The garden of Shoden-ji Temple, which also dates from the early Edo era, borrows the same Mount Hiei using the framing device of a small nearby wood. This flat dry garden, measuring just 343 square yards, is attached to the east of the *hojo*. Like *Ryoan-ji*, it

Ninna-ji Pond Garden, Kyoto, which borrows the outlines of a pagoda.

contains fifteen objects in sets of three, five and seven. Unlike *Ryoan-ji*, however, these objects are not rocks but clipped azaleas, aligned along the white-washed, tile-topped garden wall rather than distributed across the entire garden floor.

The pond garden in Ninna-ji Temple in north-west Kyoto dates from around 1690. In this case, the object "captured" is a piece of man-made architecture. Viewed from the veranda of the main hall, the temple's five-storeyed pagoda is drawn into the composition through a framework of treetops and bushes.

The new garden prototype of the Edo era: the large garden for strolling

The basic principles of spatial organization

The large garden for strolling is not strictly speaking a new garden prototype in the sense used up till now. Such is its unique nature, however, that it may nevertheless be termed a prototype. It is unique not simply in terms of scale, but in its unification of various elements of previous garden prototypes by means of a new principle of spatial organization. Its ingredients include the ponds, islands, winding streams and waterfalls of Heian boating gardens, the lakeside footpaths and hills of the smaller-scale Kamakura and Muromachi strolling gardens, the fixed indoor vantage points of Muromachi gardens as well as elements of the Momoyama tea garden.

The large garden for strolling is a secularized garden. There is no place here for Buddhist temples of any sect; the tea houses and small Shinto shrines which nevertheless occasionally appear serve decorative rather than religious purposes.

The layout of these gardens is directly related to their original function – as palace gardens for the daimyo families obliged to spend half their year in Edo. With the collapse of the feudal system at the start of the Meiji era, most of these gardens were converted into public parks – a status they continue to enjoy today.

They are all organized along the same principle: a path around the garden takes the visitor past a succes-

Dry landscape garden of Shoden-ji Temple, Kyoto, borrowing Mount Hiei from the far distance.

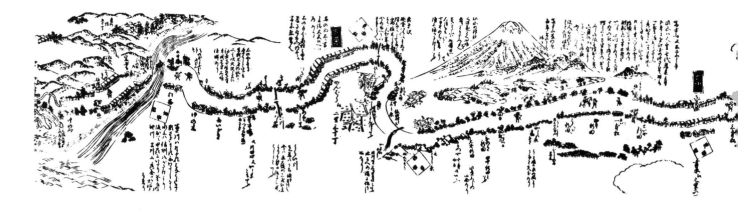

Illustration from an eighteenth-century travel guide showing the sights lining the Tokaido, the main route linking Tokyo and Kyoto. Mount Fuji appears twice, as seen from two different angles along the way.

sion of changing landscapes, re-creations of famous natural sights. Important here is that fact that these individual panaromas occur in non-hierarchical sequence, rather than building up to a single climax.

Circumambulation of a spatially-organized landscape was also the principle behind the pilgrimage circuits which arose from the twelfth century onwards. The earliest of these embraced the 33 Kannon temples in and around Kyoto, and the 88 Kannon temples on the island of Shikoku. (Kannon, or Kwannon, is a Buddhist goddess of mercy. Her powers include the protection of the faithful, the persecuted and the shipwrecked, and the abundant provision of children. – Translator's note.) Such pilgrimages were originally undertaken as a means of earning merit and thus helping ensure passage to a Buddhist paradise. In the peaceful times of the Edo era, however, the religious dimension became increasingly lost as the pilgrimage boomed into a tourist industry. Some 120 new circuits sprang up all over the country, offering "pilgrims" the chance to get away for a few days from their rigorous social duties at home.[78]

What bound these pilgrimages together into self-contained circuits was not a hierarchical route leading to an ultimate final goal, but their non-hierarchical organization around a system of magical numbers such as 33, 88 and 100. Pilgrims were to be guided not to a specific destination, but past a certain number of temples along the way, all of which were equally important. Manfred Speidel summarizes this system as follows: "The combination of the idea of holy numbers

with the idea of a diffusion of holy places with 'deities' of equal rank... resulted in the creation of homogeneous sacred spaces. This is an abstract system which works like a framework: it is transferable in order to organize other situations in the same way."[79]

Pilgrimages which had once stretched over hundreds of miles could now be reduced to fit into your own back garden. As long as the end result incorporated – in whatever form – the appropriate number of sites to be visited, such miniature-scale pilgrimages lost none of their religious efficacy. A pilgrim could thus now earn the same merit by simply ringing a temple bell cast with the images of the 33 Kannon temples as by spending three laborious weeks visiting them all in person. Speidel also mentions that a garden for strolling was built in Edo in 1782 as a small-scale copy of the famous pilgrimage circuit of the 33 Kannon temples in and around Kyoto. The garden for strolling here assumes the function of a pilgrimage route, and probably represents a last attempt to reintroduce a religious dimension into the now secularized traditions of garden architecture.

The spatial organization of the large-scale garden for strolling finds an interesting parallel in a popular board game of Edo times – *Meisho sugoroku*, the "board game of famous places". The board was organized into grids, circles and spirals of fields, each field containing one of the sights of Edo. Players advanced from one field to the next depending on the fall of the dice. Playing the game thus took them on an imaginary trip through Edo, whereby they experienced the city as a

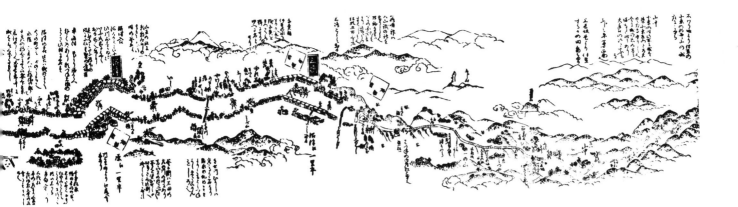

structural sequence of individual sights. Just, in fact, as they would experience a garden for strolling.[80]

It is interesting to note in this context that the *Edo meisho-zue*, a work comprising twenty volumes published between 1834 and 1836, catalogues and illustrates some one thousand famous sights in and around Edo but contains not a single overall view of the city. Edo is instead reproduced as a sequence of visually and spatially distinct events. The large number of sights listed reflects the new interest and pride of the citizens of Edo in the attractions of their home city.

The concept of recreating *meisho*, famous places, in both gardens and woodcut prints is by no means an innovation of Edo times. We have already encountered it in the Heian period, namely in the natural sights illustrated in indigenous Japanese *yamato-e* painting, and in the recommendations of the *Sakutei-ki*, the classic guide to garden-making of the eleventh century. What is new to the Edo era, however, is its understanding of space not as a continuum in which objects are contained but as a sequence of places. The garden for strolling no longer "contains" a set of symbolic or non-symbolic objects, but comprises a sequence of images and scenes. As in pilgrimage circuits and the *Meisho sugoroku* board game, so now the sequence of famous sights becomes the structural principle underlying spatial organization at all levels – from countrywide road networks to individual gardens. The same priciple gave rise to a whole new genre of literature – *meizo-zue*, "illustrated manuals of famous places" and forerunners of the tourist guides of today. Here space is

presented as an experience which is moulded by cultural learning processes, coloured by individual associations and structured by time and motion.[81]

In the gardens for strolling of the Edo era, famous sights are frequently represented by iconic, or realistic, means; in other words, they share a physical resemblance to the scenery they depict. These became known as *shukkei*, reduced-scale replicas of natural scenery. One of the best examples is the strikingly realistic miniature of Mount Fuji in Suizen-ji Park in Kumamoto. Other representations might take an indexical form; in other words, they have some literal connection to the sight they denote. Thus the famous dyke of the West Lake of Hangzhou is indicated in Tokyo's Koraku-en Park simply by a small dyke, after which all similarity with the original ends. Other representations again are of purely symbolic nature. "Symbol", according to Max Bense, "means replacement." This category includes the Yin/Yang, male/female rock formations which were highly popular in Edo times. There is here no longer either a visual or physical relationship between the original and its representative. Finally, some representations were purely imaginary portrayals of places either mythical (such as those sung about in poetry) or real (but never personally visited by the garden designer).

The sense of aesthetic unity breathed today by these gardens for strolling should not be taken to indicate that they were designed according to an overall master plan. On the contrary, they were generally created over several generations in a process of incremental plan-

185

*Hilly landscape seen from the tea arbour in
Joju-en Park. In the foreground, a stone basin
in the shape of a kimono sleeve.*

Artificial hill and sawatari-ishi stones crossing a winding stream in Koraku-en Park, Okayama.

ning. In adding his own, new contribution, each designer was thereby careful to respect the work of his predecessors and the harmony of the whole.

Components of the strolling gardens of the Edo era

Hills

Artificial hills – *tsuki-yama* – emerged as a common feature of large gardens for strolling of the Edo era. One explanation for the increase in their numbers and size may be that the daimyo nobles, on their half-yearly travels to and from Edo, fell in love with the beautiful mountain scenery along the route. This they subsequently sought to reproduce on a smaller scale in their palace gardens. Cone-shaped hills representing Mount Fuji were particularly popular. These hills can often be climbed, rewarding the effort with a commanding view of the garden. Their contours are usually rounded and soft, their surfaces grassy, and their mood open and cheerful.

Water

Artificial ponds were equally popular. They, too, radiate a sense of cheerfulness and openness. The rock-piled banks of the sunken ponds of the Momoyama era have disappeared; ponds are now shallower and often ringed by a single string of rocks. Shorelines blend gently into the surroundings, and large beaches of pebbles and sand are gone. A last example of a beach-lined

pond from this period is found within Sento Gosho Park, part of Kyoto's imperial palace. Broad, winding streams – real and dry – and artfully-placed *sawatari-ishi* testify to the skill of the designer. *Sawatari-ishi* – "steps across the marsh" – are unusually large stones laid in the riverbed. Waterfalls in these gardens are highly naturalistic and carry a small volume of water.

Islands

Islands assumed a less dramatic appearance than in the past and were crowned with fewer rock compositions;

Rock foundations for the stilts supporting
Kikugetsu-tei Pavilion in Ritsurin Park,
Takamatsu.

Rock group on a slope in the pond garden of
Chishaku-in Temple, Kyoto.

Rock composition symbolizing the Isles of the Blest in the south pond of Ritsurin park.

Naturalistic waterfall in Kako Pond in Koraku-en Park, Okayama.

in Ritsurin Park in Takamatsu, only two of the twelve islands feature rock settings. Ritsurin Park also contains the finest examples of the disappearing breed of crane and turtle rock islands. Even those that were built tended to lack the expressiveness found in the head and tail stones of their predecessors. In a further break with time-honoured tradition, they also ceased to appear as a pair: from early Edo times onwards it became common to select just one of the two. Joju-en Park in Kumamoto possesses a beautiful set of *sawatobi-ishi*, "stepping-stones across the marsh". These are large stones placed between islands or along shorelines; despite their name, they are not to be walked on, but serve purely decorative purposes.

Rockwork

Rock settings in the gardens of the Edo era decreased both in quantity and formal discipline, becoming almost casual in character. Only occasionally do we encounter a triadic rock composition near the top of a hill, or a rock group symbolizing Mount Horai near the water's edge. Rocks used as *tobi-ishi* are generally large in size, denying their modest origins in the rustic tea garden. It was fashionable in Edo times to erect Yin/Yang stones at prominent points, representing the interplay of the male and female principle. Perhaps we may see in such rockwork the counterpart to the playful eroticism of the *ukiyo-e*, the "pictures of the floating world".

Plants

With the declining significance and quality of rockwork in Edo gardens came the rise of topiary art. Ritsurin Park contains trees trimmed into box shapes, in a fashion called *hako-zukuri,* literally meaning "box-making". Not all trees were artificially trimmed: venerable pines and small, natural woods were equally popular elements of the garden landscape. Entire sections of parks were devoted to cherry and plum groves. A new feature of Edo gardens is the appearance of small rice paddies. Although these might be interpreted as a revival of one of the early archetypes of the Japanese garden, the *shinden* or "Divine Fields", it seems more likely that the inclusion of such scenes of peasants working in the rice fields was inspired by an overly romantic notion of rural life.

Paths and bridges

Only about half of the circuit through the garden now follows the water's edge. The rest passes through small groves and across hills. The large strolling gardens of the Edo era are characterized by a greater number and variety of bridges which the visitor has to cross. These bridges tend to be larger than their Momoyama predecessors; together with the pavilions, they add man-made artificial form to the man-made natural form of the garden, in a trend dating back to the Momoyama era.

*Garden scenery around the Temple of Rebirth
in Paradise in Sanzen-in Temple, Ohara, Kyoto.*

*Naturalistic rock grouping around a
shiraito-taki, a Waterfall of White Threads in
Koraku-en Park, Tokyo. Early Edo era.*

*Playfully-contrived bridge forms in Ritsurin Park
and skrubs trimmed in hako zukuri, "box style".*

Tea arbours

Tea arbours built in *so-an* style, namely as rustic tea huts, are usually tucked away in smaller rustic tea gardens of their own. Shoin-style tea arbours, on the other hand, tend to be found at the edges of ponds or winding garden streams in order to provide a rectangular frame for the view. An example here is *kikugetsu-tei* Pavilion in Ritsurin Park, which stands above the water on stilts. The architect clearly exploited the opportunity to employ particularly beautiful rocks as the foundations for the pavilion's supports.

Mirei Shigemori has characterized both the individual components of the large garden for strolling and its overall layout as "female" and "weak", and thus quite the opposite of the "male" and "strong" gardens of the preceding Momoyama era. Two and half centuries of peace have clearly left their mark in the aesthetics of the Japanese garden.

Ryu-ten, the Tea Shop by the Garden Stream in Koraku-en Park, Okayama, is a prime example of the aesthetic unio mystica of right angle and natural form. It was built in the Heian style to house the Feast by the Winding Stream.

The garden stream and stepping-stones of Hikaku-tei, the Flying Crane Garden, here cross one corner of Seiko-ken Tea Hut. The view from inside the tea hut is framed horizontally and vertically by the rectangular structure of the building.
Photo: Minao Tabata

Plan of Jiko-in and its cleverly-designed approach (Redrawn and abridged from: Shigemori, M. and K., Taikei, vol.15, 1972).

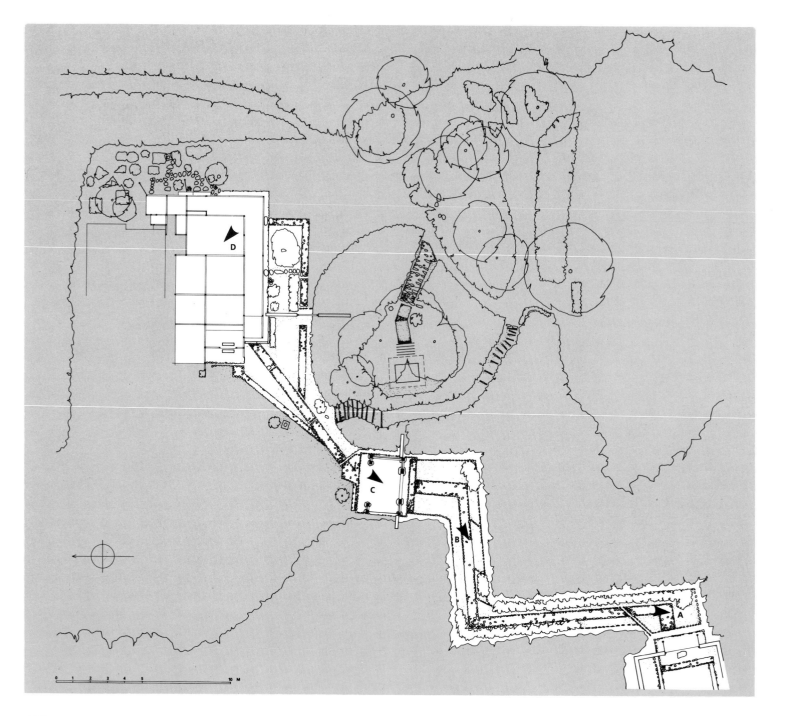

Gardens in retreats built by former samurai turned scholars, priests and tea masters

Hermitage gardens, like the gardens for strolling of the daimyo princes, combine a variety of traditional elements from the garden for strolling, the tea garden, the dry landscape garden and the *shakkei* garden. Here, however, they are brought down to a domestic scale. This is reflected in the small size of two of the most important gardens of this type: *Shisen-do*, the "Poet's Hermitage", was built by Ishikawa Jozan in Kyoto as a retreat in which to pursue his literary interests following his retirement from a samurai career; *Jiko-in*, the "Tender Light Temple", was built by Katagiri Sekishu, a former feudal lord, as a temple cum tea house retreat in Yamato Koriyama. Although their surface area is already limited, both retreats seem to "waste" half their sites on their approach routes. But it is precisely these approaches which, by means of sophisticated sensory illusions, serve to prepare the visitor for his goal, a place of stillness and meditation.

Japan is a small, narrow, densely-populated country where space, rather than time, is money. Both *Shisen-do* and *Jiko-in* are prime examples of the Japanese genius for manipulating time, space and human motion to create a convincing illusion of greater space.

We shall here be examining twelve different techniques with which our visual and haptic experience of space is thus manipulated. The first I shall call the "mouse-hole experience". It is a technique encoun-

tered at the entrance gate to *Jiko-in*, for example. Approaching from a wide expanse of open fields, we are made to pass through a relatively small space, the first gate. I see in this a conscious attempt to enlarge the visitor's experience of the space which follows. Although still small, it seems large in contrast to the compressed space of the entrance gate.

The second technique, what might be termed a "space-tunnel experience", comes into effect immediately after the first gate. From here we follow a path overshadowed on both sides by dense undergrowth.

199

The path is dark, cool and wet, and actually lies two to three feet below the rest of the garden; its overall effect is that of a tunnel. The end of the tunnel is kept out of sight. Since there is almost nothing to see, the visitor will almost automatically increase his pace. Psychologically, this faster pace will produce the feeling of having walked a greater distance than that actually covered.

A third technique used to create the impression of wider space could be called the "zigzag-progression experience". Two zigzag turns are introduced along the dark, tunnel-like path. This artificial detour in turn increases the distance that seems to separate the start and end of the path.

After the second zigzag bend, we are suddenly brought up short by a larger, brighter space with a view of a two-storeyed castle gate. This I call the "stopping-space experience".

The fifth technique is revealed in the second gate which now confronts us. Rather like a game of "Snakes and Ladders", where players suddenly find themselves right back at the start, we now have to enter the garden all over again.

The sixth technique is one of "contrast experience". Passing through the second gate after the long dark tunnel, we find ourselves in an open, light space with a view of our goal, *Jiko-in*. More accurately speaking, it is only a partial view of the double gables of its thatched hipped roofs. Here the seventh technique takes effect: presented with a choice of three possible routes, our hesitation is itself a "slowing-down experience".

The eighth technique, the "cave experience", comes with our entry into *Jiko-in* itself. The actual entrance area, the *genkan* or "dark barrier", is again dark and disorienting, and frustrates our eager expectations one last time.

In order to enter the *shoin*, we must undergo a widespread Japanese ritual comprising the ninth and tenth techniques. The first of these is a "floating experience" as we step upwards onto a higher level, from where our elevated angle again enriches and enlarges our perception of space. The second, "direct-touch experience" comes with the removal of our shoes before we step onto the tatami mats covering the floor.

Having reached our goal, we now encounter the eleventh technique, the "*shakkei* experience" supplied by the view – framed by the eaves above and the veranda below – of the small dry landscape garden outside. In addition to clipped azalea bushes in the shape of hills, the composition "captures alive" the chain of eight famous peaks on the distant eastern edge of the Yamato basin.

Shisen-do in Kyoto employs an additional technique at this point, whereby spatial illusion is reinforced with auditory effects. The constant babble of a nearby waterfall, and the occasional detonations of a *shishi-odoshi* "deer scare", both add to our sense of depth. The rhythmical sound of a bamboo see-saw hitting a stone and discharging its water brings to mind the Zen saying: "Not the stillness in stillness, but the stillness in movement is the real stillness."

In view of the very different nature of the last experience now enjoyed, I hesitate to number it as the twelfth in the sequence we have just detailed. It is namely an esoteric technique. In our journey through *Jiko-in* garden we have seen its creator, Sekishu, as master architect and gardener; now we meet him as mystic. In *Jiko-in shoin* our bodies seem to float in space and our vision to extend for miles, and we pause and are still. It is a feeling experienced by almost every visitor. We are invited to meditate, to experience the vastness of inner space. We slowly cease to perceive

the outside world, and in doing so relinquish the awareness of self. We are thus made aware of awareness, which is empty and hence the ultimate extension of space. Only a place inducing such an experience – or more accurately, "non-experience" – may truly be called a temple, since only here do we gain an insight into who we truly are.

The techniques described above naturally owe much to the "passageway" ritual which Sen no Rikyu created for the rustic tea garden. But they then go further by incorporating features from other types of garden. Katagiri Sekishu, creator of *Jiko-in*, was Kobori Enshu's successor as the "high priest" of tea. The tea rooms attached to the *shoin* testify to his skill in this art, too.

The naturalistic scenery of the large gardens for strolling of the Edo era: the south pond of Ritsurin Park with a wooden bridge spanning the foreground.

Rock settings on the Heavenly Maiden Island in the south pond of Ritsurin Park.

Edo attitudes towards nature and garden design

Aesthetic ideals of the Edo era and their influence upon garden design

As we have already observed, the small pond garden and the dry landscape garden continued to be built throughout the Edo era in stereotypical forms of older archetypes. Most are attached to Buddhist temples. In their overall layout, their rockwork and their vegetation, however, they lose the discipline and expressiveness of their predecessors. They were executed in standardized fashion, lacking poetry, depth, even beauty. For the essence of beauty lies in transcending the conventional. But Edo gardens simply imitate the styles of earlier eras, and not nature itself – whether in its outward forms, its inner essence or its mode of operation.

The large gardens for strolling of the daimyo nobles adopt numerous elements of previous garden prototypes and combine them into a new design solution, namely the path which leads the visitor past a seemingly endless chain of "famous sights", a string of pearls both real and imaginary. This revised formula had the power to extract new meaning from familiar garden scenery.

The garden for strolling is a secularized garden. Its outward appearance grows increasingly more realistic and naturalistic, albeit with the exceptions of the rather grotesque Yin/Yang, male/female rock groups and occasional instances of daimyo ostentation. For to shatter a huge rock into some ninety pieces, haul these into a garden and then cement them all back together again – as was done in Koraku-en Park in Okayama – is surely an act of bravura rather than art. Because of the preference for large-scale naturalistic landscapes, architecture was relegated somewhat to the background. Even those original buildings no longer standing must have played an only secondary role. The trend towards more naturalistic scenery is reflected in the widespread use of winding streams both feeding and linking ponds, as well as in the introduction of groves of pine, plum and cherry trees as independent sub-gardens within the whole.

The aesthetic ideals of the middle and late Edo era are those of the *chonin*, the townspeople, and above all the newly-rich merchant classes. Characteristic of these new Edo ideals of an urban mass culture are the following: *iki* – chic stylishness with an erotic undertone; *share* – sophistication, sense of humour; *shibumi* – taste, refinement; *tsu* – informedness, professionalism; and finally *asobi* – playfulness in the arts and crafts.

Nature no longer contains a divine, cosmic or mystic message for the artist to discover and then express through garden scenery. The garden is simply a stage set, artfully decorated with the latest in sophisticated and fashionable props. The large garden for strolling of the Edo era is like a catalogue of garden fashions, offering not only an endless selection of famous sights but an imaginative range of bridge forms and shrubbery "coiffures".

203

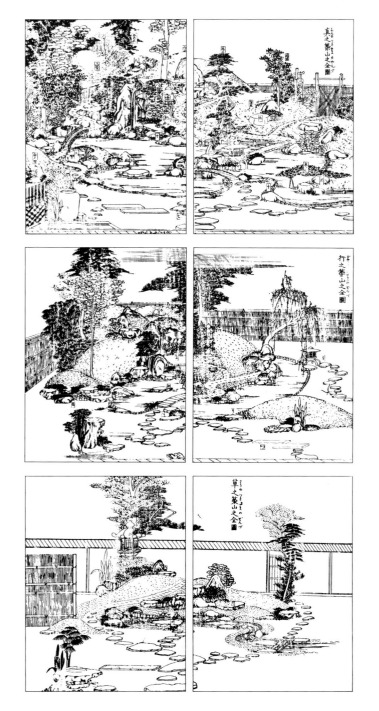

Secret transmissions of garden art and new illustrated manuals of garden design

The two gardens of *Shisen-do* in Kyoto and *Jiko-in* near Nara are closely related to academic Chinese *bunjin* painting. This *bunjin* tradition is similarly reflected in a secret garden text composed in 1680 by the print-maker and man of letters Hishikawa Morono-bu, entitled *Yokei tsukuri niwa no zu*, "Garden Drawings for the Creation of Specific Views". In this single volume he suggests eighteen ways of creating gardens having particular atmospheres, in double-page illustrations employing the sophisticated drawing techniques of the day. At the top of each illustration he describes the scenic ingredients necessary to create the garden in question – whether famous sights in China or Japan, seasonal scenery or poetic lore -, and thereby falls fully in line with the secret oral traditions of Japanese garden art.

By the second half of the Edo era, gardens were no longer the exclusive privilege of daimyo nobles and samurai warriors but became equally the domain of the *chonin*, the townspeople. Thus the demand grew for experienced gardeners, and particularly for those in possession of *kuden*, highly-prized oral transmissions of the secrets of garden design. This new breed of professionals, called *niwa-shi*, or "garden masters", now supplied the townspeople not only with the artistic designs for their gardens, but also with the materials and decorative elements required in their construction, such as rocks, trees and stone lanterns. Even the *niwa-shi*,

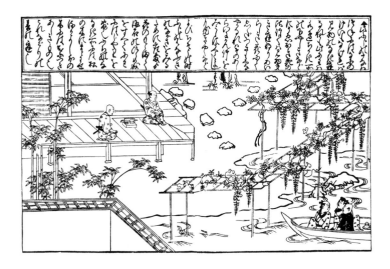

"A garden scenery to remind one of spring." The garden's main features are a wisteria-draped pergola near the water's edge and a few pines in the background. An illustration from Hishikawa Moronobu's "Yokei tsukuri niwa no zu" of 1680.

however, proved unable to match the rising demand for gardening expertise; another solution had to be found. This was to take the form of a new branch of literature – practical garden manuals which could be sold cheaply and in large quantities thanks to the newly-developed techniques of woodcut printing.

The results were not altogether satisfactory. Such manuals destroyed the spirit of individual creativity and innovation in garden art and led to general artistic stagnation. By describing garden architecture in terms of rigid stylistic categories, they inevitably encouraged the same fixity in reality, too. Perhaps the most widely-read "do-it-yourself" manual of this type was Enkin Kitamura's *Tsukiyama teizo-den*, "Transmission of Making Mountains and Creating Gardens", written in 1735. In addition to practical advice on how to create garden scenery, it devotes an entire section to woodcuts of famous gardens of old, such as the Golden Pavilion and *Daisen-in*. A second volume was published in 1828 by Ritoken Akisato under the same title, and the two were subsequently sold as a set. Akisato carries the strict classification of gardens and their components even further than his predecessors: everything in the book is now discussed in terms of standardized types. Although beautifully illustrated, these books reflect less the creative spirit of the *niwa-shi,* the professional garden masters, than the commercial spirit of the *ueki-ya* gardening businesses.

This trend towards oversimplification in garden art is typically demonstrated in the distinction introduced between the flat and the hilly garden. Having settled for one or the other, the would-be garden-maker then faces a further choice of three possible styles, each differing in the elaboration of its details. Using the Muromachi terms derived originally from the Sino-Japanese art of calligraphy and subsequently applied to other arts, these three styles are entitled *shin*, highly formal, *gyo*, semi-formal, and *so*, informal or simplified. Such distinctions between flat and hilly, between formal, semi-formal and informal, imply a progressive reduction in the number of compositional elements used within a garden and an increasing informality in its overall design. But whether this was simply a standard design practice inherited from earlier times, or whether it was indeed the result of literary simplifications in the Edo era, must remain in question.

The carver and the carved
Gardens as mindscapes

The gardens of the Meiji era refer initially to the traditional stereotypes of the dry landscape garden, pond garden and tea garden of Edo times. The fifth new garden prototype, which emerged at the start of the twentieth century, was initially dominated by carved natural rocks; these were later joined by synthetic materials. This prototype no longer starts from existing models in nature, but is better understood as an intellectual projection onto nature. Its gardens are thus no longer *land*-scapes but *mind*-scapes.

Since the Second World War the Japanese garden has established its new territory within the courtyards and entrances of local government offices, cultural halls, museums, corporate headquarters and public piazzas. Its creators are now sculptors, architects and university-trained professional landscape designers. The garden which has developed since the Meiji Restoration is a statement of man's independence of nature, and of his desire to superimpose upon nature his own egoistic will.

From the Meiji era to the present

With the signing of the friendship treaty between Japan and the United States of America by Commodore Matthew Perry in 1854, over two hundred years of Tokugawa isolationism came to an end. The Americans were given permission to establish consular offices in Japan.

Westernization versus traditionalism

For the Tokugawa shoguns, the arrival of the Americans spelled the end of their lengthy rule. Younger members of the traditional samurai class saw the signing of the friendship treaty as an act of capitulation, proof that the present shogunate was incapable of expelling the foreign barbarian. A royalist coup in Kyoto in 1866 led to the restoration of the emperor to full powers. The shogunate capitulated; by 1867, and after remarkably little bloodshed, the reins of power were firmly back in the hands of emperor Meiji Tenno (1852-1912).

Japan's new leaders, young samurai activists and Kyoto courtiers, soon revised their attitudes towards the outside world. They silently dropped their calls for the expulsion of the "barbarians" and instead abolished the feudal land system and the territorial powers of the daimyo lords, thereby ending Japan's rigid class system. They dissolved the samurai class altogether and accepted that all citizens were equal before the law. In the 1870s they solidly endorsed the policy of

bummei kaika, of adopting Western "Civilization and Enlightenment". Edo was renamed Tokyo, capital of the east, and made the seat of the emperor.

The new Meiji constitution, modelled on German theories of government, was proclaimed in 1889. Its language remained highly traditionalist; the emperor was enshrined as divine head of the *kokutai*, "the body of the country". This national body was in turn envisaged as an obedient Confucian state held together by the patriarchal and sacrosanct institution of the emperor. Tokyo Imperial University became a sort of educational funnel for orthodox government officials. It was not until New Year's Day 1946 that Emperor Hirohito abrogated his divine descent and declared himself a human being.

Japanese culture of the Meiji era was strongly oriented towards Western models. Thus, for example, Japanese architects adopted both building styles and construction materials from the West. They were encouraged in this by the government itself, since it was hoped the new architecture would help counter the problem of the fires which regularly devastated Japanese cities, which at that time comprised mainly single – and two-storeyed wooden houses. Western influence stretched to other spheres, too, including literature. Almost all the famous Western works of both prose and poetry were translated into Japanese. Japanese authors subsequently sought to compose their own works along Western lines. The only Western painting previously to have reached Japan had accompanied the Jesuits in the sixteenth century and the Dutch in the seventeenth. From now on, all the major European art trends from the eighteenth century onwards were to find their way to Japan.

This intensive infatuation with the culture and values of the West quickly served to highlight what Varley has called "the vexing problem of individualism in modern Japan" – in other words, the difficulty of reconciling the newly-discovered fascination with "the innermost psychological and emotional life of the individual" with a society which still officially stressed filial piety, obedience to the group and loyalty to the emperor.[82] The Japanese language did not even have a word for individualism or privacy.

But the quest for Western-style individuality was soon thwarted by the advent of a new form of conformity, namely a mass culture determined not by an ethical code but by the products of mechanization: masstransportation, massproduction, massconsumption, massmedia. Powerful corporate enterprises, aided by the sustained growth of the economy since the Second World War, now dictate virtually every aspect of consumer life. They manipulate the life of the "individual" from the cradle to the grave.

The garden in Meiji, Taisho and Showa times

In 1871 a law was passed in Japan which declared large numbers of temple and daimyo gardens from Momoyama and Edo times to be public parks. Many of these gardens had fallen into disrepair and required restoration. Such work was carried out by people who had been sent to Europe to study its parks; the end product was often a strange marriage of traditional Japanese and European gardens, particularly in the case of the large daimyo gardens for strolling, which were closest in scale to their European counterparts. The problem was compounded by the poor level of scholarship in the history of the Japanese garden. The magnificent models of the past, the gardens of Kyoto, no longer attracted the visitors of former times, and were allowed to deteriorate. Indeed, their most important components – rocks, stone lanterns – were often sold to raise money. Scholarly research had similarly come to a standstill. Although Shigemori documents no less than eighty different books on the Japanese garden published during the Meiji era, he dismisses all of them as superficial and ill-informed, if not downright childish. These were mainly cheap do-it-yourself manuals or equally unreliable descriptions of existing gardens by authors who had made no effort to actually visit them in person.[83]

Although thirteen Departments of Landscaping were founded at various universities in different prefectures, they were all subordinate to the faculties of either Agriculture, Forestry or Horticulture. The subjects covered by these departments were predominantly concerned with Western landscape design. There were no courses on the history of the Japanese garden, nor was research in this field encouraged.

To put it bluntly, Japanese garden architecture was no longer considered an art. "Tracking the models skilful masters have left behind", as the *Sakutei-ki* of Heian times had recommended, was deemed obsolete in a climate of Western-style "Civilization and Enlightenment". The gardens built by commercial *ueki-ya*, "tree trimmers" or "tree growers", had neither underlying concepts, symbolic content nor recognizable themes. They were merely statements of the level of taste and size of purse of the people who paid for them.

The ancient Japanese art of *ishi wo tateru*, "erecting rocks", and the later "ishi-gumi", "rock composition", degenerated into *sute-ishi*, "discarding rocks", which meant no more than their naturalistic distribution.

Meiji gardens are usually attached to private residences, in a curious return to the original function of the garden in Heian times, when it bore a direct relation to the patterns of daily life and formed an integral part of the home, albeit a princely one.

Of the many books on the Japanese garden published during the Taisho era (1912–1926), Shigemori singles out just four or five authors whose works awakened new interest in indigenous Japanese garden art.

The predominant trend in the arts world-wide at this time was naturalism, and its influence was to colour Japanese garden architecture from Meiji times right up to the present. Gardens were now expected to be truthful copies of nature in its "real" form. They were no longer "nature as art", nature designed and moulded by human hands, but simply a part of nature made by nature. The selective, reductive, abstractive hand of the designer was to remain hidden so that garden might appear a perfect icon of nature. This attitude remained more or less unchanged until the revival of the *kare-sansui* in the early Showa era and the birth of the most recent garden prototype. Only then did abstraction and symbolism resume their place within the Japanese garden.

Stereotypical forms of the Meiji pond garden

In terms of their overall layout, the pond gardens of the Meiji era resemble those of the middle and late Edo era. No new variations were invented. Shigemori distinguishes between four standard types of layout. The first takes the form of the Sino-Japanese character for "water", the second the shape of a sweet potato (thick in the middle, thin at each end), the third the shape of a worm (thin and winding) and the fourth a predominantly concave form.[84]

*Rock setting at the conflux of the two streams
in the garden of Murin-an Villa, Kyoto.*

The garden of Murin-an Villa

In 1896, prince and veteran statesman Aritomo Yama-gata built himself a villa in the district of *Kusagawa-cho* at the foot of Kyoto's eastern mountains. His gardener was Jihei Ogawa. Kusagawa-cho, which lies not far from Nanzen-ji Temple, subsequently developed into an exclusive suburb of expensive villas. The completion of a canal between Lake Biwa and the city in 1890 ensured plentiful supplies of fresh water, undoubtedly contributing to the popularity of the district.

The garden of Murin-an Villa falls into Shigemori's "sweet potato" category: narrow at both ends and broad in the middle. Aligned along an east-west axis, and with two ponds in the middle, its function is that of a garden for strolling. Its outer appearance is highly naturalistic, but it reproduces none of the famous na-tural sights found in the large daimyo gardens of Edo times. Like most of the gardens in the district, it makes superb use of *shakkei*, "borrowing" the eastern moun-tains into the garden composition through a gap in the woods surrounding the garden. Immediately below this gap, at the eastern end of the garden, lies a three-stepped naturalistic waterfall. Its waters run into a gar-den stream, which flows over rapids into the first pond and from there to the second.

This first stream is joined near the *shoin* by a second, arriving from the northern end of the garden. A bridge of hewn stone crossing the lower section of the stream offers a contemplative view of the rock setting marking the confluence of the two streams. The lower part of the garden is generously provided with lawns, some of them featuring horizontal rock compositions. These rocks number among the visual delights lining the path which takes the visitor around the naturalistic sequence of stream – pond – pond – stream. In many ways the garden echoes the small-scale pond gardens of Edo times. It is one of the most delightful gardens of the Meiji era.

The naturalistic garden of Murin-an Villa from 1896, framed by the sliding screens of the shoin. The "borrowed" eastern mountains in the background are veiled by the autumn mist.

212

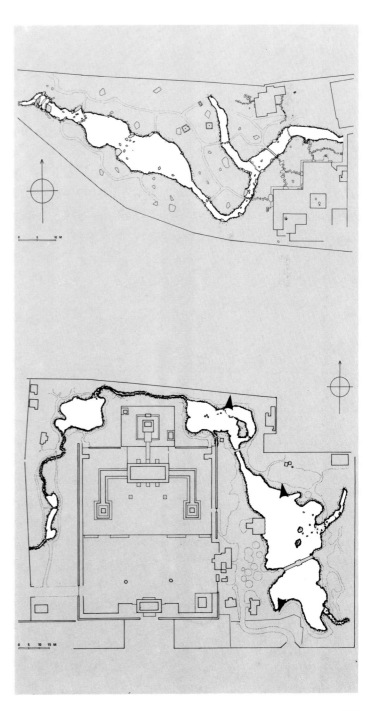

Above:
A naturalistic pond garden of the Meiji era:
Murin-an, Kyoto, dating from 1896.
Plan of the grounds.

Below:
The pond garden at the Heian Shrine in Kyoto,
from 1895. Plan of the grounds.

The Heian Shrine garden

The Heian Shrine was completed in 1895. It is dedicated
to Kammu Tenno, founder of Heian-kyo, the original
Kyoto. There were two reasons for building the shrine:
to commemorate the 1100th anniversary of the founding of Heian-kyo, and to console its citizens for the fact
that Meiji Tenno had since moved the capital to Tokyo.
It was planned as a small-scale replica of the *Chodo-in*,
the Hall of State originally located within the precincts
of the Heian imperial palace. But it proved a task beyond the architects of the Meiji era; their inadequate
historical knowledge of Heian architecture meant that
neither the buildings nor the garden of the complex
successfully captured the true spirit of Heian times.
There was another problem too: the notion of recreating a Hall of State as the setting for a Shinto shrine im-
plied a fundamental change of function: the secular
must become religious. Outdoors the situation was reversed: the garden was conceived not as a sacred landscape of divine islands floating in divine ponds, but as a
large and decidedly secular park in which the general
public could take a stroll after worshipping at the
shrine. Here, too, the designer was Jihei Ogawa, who
chose a highly naturalistic solution featuring a large variety of trees and flowers and thereby guaranteeing
visual attractions at all times of year. The nearby eastern mountains are again "borrowed" for the composition whenever possible. The garden ultimately belongs
to the strolling-garden type rather than to the shrine
and palace gardens of Heian times.

The garden covers an area of five acres, divided into a western, a central and an eastern section. The western garden is famous for the hanging cherry and willow trees which surround its small pond. The northern end of the pond contains a six-foot-high naturalistic waterfall and a small peninsula. The chief attraction of the central garden is a pond with a number of rock islands and the now famous *sawatari-ishi*, "steps across the marsh", made of pier stones from Kyoto's Gojo bridge. From here the water flows into an eastern pond which – highly unusual for its day – features both a crane and a turtle island, as well as a long, covered bridge which frames the view of the garden. The garden to the south is a recent addition by Kinsaku Nakane; with the abundant rock settings along its banks, it stands in clear contrast to the rest of the Heian Shrine garden, which contains almost no rockwork worthy of note.

Stereotypical forms of the dry landscape garden since the Meiji era

Mirei Shigemori estimates that only one third of all the gardens created from Meiji to early Showa times were *kare-sansui* gardens. He gives forty-two of them in his "Taikei"[85]. Stagnation had set into dry landscape garden design even in the late Edo era, and from then on *kare-sansui* gardens became little more than pond gardens without water. It was a genre which somehow failed to suit Meiji tastes, which were oriented towards the naturalistic landscape compositions which *kare-sansui* by definition could not supply; as an independent garden form with its own content and compositional laws, its abstraction and symbolism could not be further from naturalistic reproduction. It was not until the advent of the Showa era (1926-1988) that Japan saw a renaissance of the "real" *kare-sansui*; this was due in part to the fact that many new temple gardens were created during this period, and in part to the influence and activities of Mirei Shigemori, the great Japanese garden artist and garden historian.

Shigemori lists 120 *kare-sansui* gardens created during the early Showa era. Characteristic features of

*View of the new garden to the south. In the
background, the covered bridge of the east
garden.*

These sawatari-ishi "steps across the marsh" in the garden of the Heian Shrine stem from the piers of Kyoto's Gojo Bridge.

Tofuku-ji Temple in Kyoto: a modern kare-sansui garden designed by Mirei Shigemori in 1940. Here the main south garden in front of the hojo; its five grass-covered knolls symbolize the five most important Buddhist temples of the Kamakura era.

Above:
One of the four different kare-sansui gardens surrounding the main abbot's quarters in Tofuku-ji Temple.

Below:
Plan of the garden.

these gardens include the new and rich variety of patterns raked into their sands and new principles of rock composition. Rocks are now chiefly placed in the vertical position, with sharp-edged mountain rocks preferred to smoothly-rounded river stones.[86]

Tofuku-ji Temple Garden

In 1880 a fire destroyed both the *hojo*, the abbot's living quarters, and several other lesser buildings within the *Tofuku-ji* temple complex. Rebuilding took place in 1889. In 1940, Mirei Shigemori was commissioned to redesign the gardens surrounding the rebuilt *shoin* in the spirit of the Kamakura era from which the temple originally dates. He chose four different types and sizes of dry garden scenery for the four different sides of the *shoin*. Of all the gardens Shigemori designed during his life, Tofuku-ji best illustrates his central role in Japanese garden history at the moment of transition from the stereotypical reproduction of traditional garden themes and scenery, the modern prototype of garden, that step into the unknown where the gardener functions effectively as sculptor.

The main south garden (A) in front of the *shoin* still processes traditional themes, but in a remarkably bold manner. The garden is divided into two halves by a diagonal. Its eastern section features four distinct rock groups; while somewhat reminiscent of traditional Mount Horai compositions, their verticality is nevertheless unprecedented. The western half of the south garden is dominated by five man-made knolls symbo-

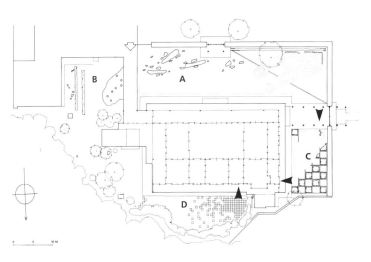

Rock settings recalling the Mount Horai
motif in the south garden of Tofuku-ji Temple,
Kyoto. The five artificial knolls can be seen
in the background.

lizing the five most important Buddhist temples of Kamarakura times, of which *Tokufu-ji* was itself one.

The other three gardens around the *shoin* break more radically with *kare-sansui* tradition. The chief compositional element is the hewn stone, while geometry provides the spatial infrastructure. The eastern garden (B), separated from the main garden by a raised, covered walkway, is a dry garden containing seven round stones – originally the foundation stones of bridge piers – in the configuration of the Big Dipper. The western garden (C), separated from the main south garden by an open corridor at ground level, reveals a chequer-board composition whose fields, 6 x 6 feet square, are alternately filled with clipped *satsuki* shrubbery or spread with white sand. The fields taper off towards the *hojo* into a white surface of raked sand. The northern garden is an elongated dry garden in which squared stepping-stones are embedded at irregular intervals in a surface of either moss or sand. A clipped hedge borders the side of the garden running along the wall (D).

In both of these last two gardens Shigemori offers a new variation upon the Japanese gardener's enduring fascination with the interplay of right angle and natural form. But since the skilled personnel needed to maintain Shigemori's dry gardens are lacking, these two gardens today present a sadly unattractive sight.

Stereotypical forms of the Meiji tea garden

The grounds of both *Murin-an* Villa and the Heian Shrine also included rustic tea gardens, and Shigemori lists over sixty-three such *roji* built during Meiji, Taisho and Showa times. None of these were designed as independent tea gardens such as those of the Momoyama and early Edo eras, but are found attached to the luxurious homes of the rich. The Meiji era lacked the great tea masters needed to create tea arbours and tea gardens, and thus *roji* were simply executed "in the style of" Rikyu, Oribe or Enshu. It is therefore impossible to treat the tea garden as a category of garden in its own right, but only as a component of other forms of garden.

Isui-en

Isui-en Garden lies south-west of Todai-ji Temple in Nara. It falls into two parts, clearly distinguishable in both scenery and style. The lower, western section features a round pond with crane and turtle islands in front of the *Sanshu-tei*, the "Pavilion of the Three Beauties". This part of the garden was first built in the 1670s by an influential Nara tanner.

The larger, eastern garden was added in 1890 by Tojiro Seki, a wealthy Nara merchant. It employs perhaps the most outstanding example of *shakkei* in the entire Meiji era. The view from *Hyoshin-tei*, the "Pavilion of the Frozen Heart", borrows not only Nara's three famous mountains of Wakakusa, Kasuga and Mikasa,

but also the upper part of the large South Gate of the Great Buddha Temple. The pond in front of *Hyoshin-tei* takes the form of the Sino-Japanese character for "water"; it contains a small island reached by a set of millstones used as stepping-stones. The garden is laid out as a garden for strolling, with some artificial hills and a three-stepped naturalistic waterfall spanned by a bridge towards its eastern end. Typically for Meiji times, rockwork is replaced almost entirely by clipped azaleas. The garden blends naturally into the real nature it "borrows".

Between these two gardens lies a tea garden with two small tea arbours, separated by a path of attractive stepping-stones and an elegant gate. In front of the *Teisho-ken* tea arbour, which has a surface area of four and a half tatami mats (nine square yards), a stone bridge crosses the garden stream to connect the other two gardens. The modesty of this small rustic tea garden contrasts with the generous scale of the *shakkei* garden to the east.

The upper pond garden of Isui-en, seen from the shoin. Millstones serve as stepping-stones across the pond. The garden makes outstanding use of shakkei: both the South Gate of the Great Buddha Temple and the mountains in the background are "borrowed" into the composition.

*Composition of rectangular and natural forms
in the dry garden north of the shoin in
Tofuku-ji Temple, Kyoto.*

*Tsubo-niwa, the small inner garden within the
grounds of Murin-an Villa, Kyoto.
Photo: Minao Tabato*

Composition of rough-hewn rocks.

Below:
*Plan of the piazza in front of the Kagawa
Prefectural Government Offices in Takamatsu.
The garden was designed by the Kenzo Tange
architectural office in 1958.*

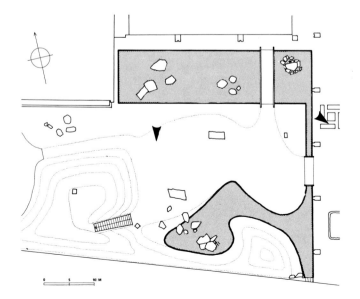

The contemporary prototype: gardens as mindscapes

The new garden prototype which emerged after the Second World War could not have been more different from its predecessors. Everything had changed – from the social background of its sponsors to the themes and elements of its composition. Its architectural settings were now the inner courtyards and entrance areas of municipal and prefectural government offices, Western-style hotels, museums, cultural halls, corporate headquarters and public piazzas.

Most of these gardens share the carved rock as their main compositional component and geometry as their spatial infrastructure. The new garden prototype is the mirror not of nature but of the will of the artist, for whom the garden becomes a vehicle of individual self-expression. The new garden artists are now sculptors, architects and landscape designers with university qualifications. Their training covers both Japanese traditions and international influences. Gardens themselves are largely abstract and are often closer in character to living sculptures. Since their compositions are not to be found in real nature, but are products of the imagination, they have been termed "mindscapes".

These gardens fall recognizably in line with Japanese tradition in their continuing pursuit of what we have earlier termed the Japanese sense of beauty: the *unio mystica* of unique, random form – no longer merely adopted from nature but invented by the mind – with the rational geometry of the right angle.

The right angle versus the hand-carved form.

been hewn into approximate sculptural forms and then combined into decorative compositions. But this is precisely what we see in the water basin, measuring some 10 x 40 yards, in Kenzo Tange's garden. The dramatic impact of this modern interplay of right angle and sculpted form is further amplified by the fact that the entire composition is reflected in the huge glass panels of the entrance hall. A curvilinear pond at the southern edge of the piazza similarly serves to accentuate the straight lines of the water basin.

In 1961, sculptor Masayuki Nagare went a step further in imposing his artistic will upon his rock material. In one of the gardens attached to the Palace Hotel in Tokyo, he places a rectangular-carved waterfall sculpture into a rectangular water basin. Formally subject to the artist's will, the rock now has only its rough surface texture with which to express its natural quality and thereby counterpoint the right angles of the artist's design.

In 1975, inspired by traditional kimono designs, Mirei Shigemori created a garden based on a complex geometry of spirals. Raked pebble patterns on a spiral motif dominate the dry part of the garden, while spirals of carved stone edgings in the pond garden are set against the natural forms of rock and gravel and the rectangular lines of the architecture.

Just as synthetic materials were finding their way into other fields of visual art, so they gradually filtered into Japanese garden design, too. Metal and plastic, although not the ready-mades of nature, may still count as "natural" materials, with man – the midwife

The pond garden attached to the south of the Kagawa Prefectural Government Offices was designed by the Kenzo Tange architectural office in 1958, and functions both as a public piazza and as a stage for open-air performances. It marks the start of a new relationship between man and garden, between the creator and the created, now within the context of international modern art. Stone-carving had, it is true, been introduced into Japanese garden architecture with the stepping-stones, stone lanterns and water basins of the Momoyama era. Never before, however, had rocks

Waterfall of hewn rocks concealing a grotto bar in the garden of the Hotel Sheraton Grande.

Geometry as spatial infrastructure: in the garden which Mirei Shigemori designed in 1975 for the Yuzen Kimono Dyeing Union Headquarters in Kyoto, spiral configurations of dressed stone are combined with the forms of natural rock and gravel.

The winding garden stream, one of the oldest
elements of Japanese garden architecture,
in the new setting of Shonandai Culture Centre
in Fujizawa. Metal trees are "planted" along its
banks. The garden was designed in 1989 by
Itsuko Hasegawa.

at their birth – delivering them into garden art. The immediate question was to find appropriate forms in which to employ these inherently amorphous and pliable materials within Japanese garden architecture.

Architect Itsuko Hasegawa talks of the creation of a "second nature" in her 1989 design for the Shonandai Culture Centre in Fujisawa. The chief compositional element of this highly-acclaimed garden is, remarkably, a winding stream, and thus one of the oldest elements of the Japanese garden. The banks of the stream are "planted" with stylized metal trees. The aesthetics remain that of the right angle versus "natural" form, but one is tempted to ask why her "second nature" stays tied to the landscape forms of "first nature" rather than seeking to express a mindscape. The search for a fully-fledged form of synthetic garden has nevertheless clearly begun. Remembering that concrete architecture began by imitating the forms of wood and stone, it comes as no surprise to see the first examples of plastic gardens similarly imitating natural forms. A case in point is the beautifully-proportioned waterfall in the lobby of the ANA Hotel in Kyoto. Its naturalistic appearance is deceptive, as the hollowness of its sound makes clear: the waterfall is in fact moulded plastic. In Hiroshi Murai's "Cool Garden" from the early 1970s, set in an all-marble courtyard in the Longchamp Textile Company in Kyoto, plastic sculptures are replaced by dried trees sprayed with silver paint.

The "Cool Garden" designed by Hiroshi Murai in the marble-lined inner courtyard of the Longchamp Textile Company, Kyoto. The trees are no longer made of synthetic material, but are "real" trees which have been dried and sprayed silver.

Contemporary attitudes towards nature and garden design

It is certainly no coincidence that the carved rock should emerge as the central compositional element in the Japanese garden at precisely the same time as the Japanese natural environment was being destroyed by industry, urban overspill and the excesses of consumer behaviour.

Why should the natural form of a rock be "destroyed" before it is used in the garden? Japanese architect Kenzo Tange an American-Japanese sculptor Isamu Noguchi offer their own answers. In an article entitled "The Secret of the Rock" written in the early 1960s, Kenzo Tange explains: "We like the carved rock, because it reflects the will of the carver. Neither the natural rocks nor the way they had been placed (in the traditional garden) reflected the slightest trace of human personality. They simply lay quietly where they were, disturbing nothing and giving no hint of a human urge to create something beautiful." Shortly before his death in 1989, the famous sculptor Isamu Naguchi stated in a interview: "The garden is made from a collaboration with nature. Man's hands are hidden by time and by many effects of nature, moss and so forth, so you are hidden. I don't want to be hidden. I want to show, therefore, I am modern. I am not a traditional *Ueki-ya,* tree trimmer."[87]

The words of both artists reveal a dualism between man and nature previously unknown in Japanese garden architecture, and the desire to impose upon nature the supposedly distinct will of man. This is the ultimate fruit of the Western-style individualism imported into Japan from Meiji times onwards, an intellectual development founded upon the deep-seated Judeo-Christian belief in the ontological distinction between nature and man, and the division of man into body and soul. In this context it is interesting to note that the therme of the 1990 International Flower Exposition in Osaka was the "Coexistence of Man and Nature", implying their inherent separateness.

We are a ready discovering to our cost the consequences of such dualistic thinking. Practised on a global scale, it brings uncheckable exploitation, deforestation and the pollution of our planet, and ultimately to "The End of Nature", to quote the title of a reccent book by Bill McKibben. With the premenitory foresight of all great art, the latest Japanese garden prototype reveals the attitude of modern man to nature, and its inevitable consequences.

With our present knowledge of the catastrophic ecological disasters ahead, it is templing to specualte upon the possible shape of a future garden prototype. I see it perhaps as a jungle, an artificial jungle terminding us of our oneness with nature. We have learned the hard way that we cannot exploit or harm nature without hurting ourselves. In the words of Osho, an Eastern mystic: "You cannot go against nature. Who wants to go against it? You are nature."[88]

A purely scientific understanding of the unity of all life in the universe is not sufficient to pievent man from destroying nature and himself. Such unity must be understood a experiental fact. There is only one path which leads to such insight: meditation.

Notes

1 Nitschke, G.: Shime, 1974 and 1988
2 Shigemori, M., 1967
3 Tsukushi, N., 1964
4 Kloetzli, R., 1983, p.3
5 ibid., pp.24-43
6 c.f. Eliade, M., 1961, p.129
7 summarized from: Ledderose, L., 1983, p.168 f.
8 Aston, W.G., 1956, p.368
9 Kloetzli, R., 1983, p.99
10 Ledderose, L., 1983, p.165
11 Slawson, D., 1987, p.97
12 Ambasz, E., 1969, p.69
13 Aston, W.G., 1956, p.190
14 ibid., p.306
15 ibid., p.315
16 ibid., p.389
17 ibid., p.145
18 ibid., p.154
19 Varley, P., 1973, p.21
20 Sierksma, F., p.90
21 c.f. Porkert, 1974, p.2
22 Kuck, L., 1968, p.91
23 Itoh, T., 1984, pp.25-27
24 Shigemori, M., 1973, vol.2, p.85
25 c.f. Morris, I., 1964, p.113
26 quoted from: Seidensticker, 1976
27 Kuitert, W., 1988, p.48 f
28 Ienaga, S., 1973, p.52
29 Morris, I., 1964, p.196
30 Tamura, T., 1964, p.177
31 Tanaka, M., 1966, pp.14-30
32 Williams, C., 1974, p.185
33 Kuitert, W., 1988, p.91
34 Shigemori, M. and K.: Taikei, vol.5, p.55
35 Kuck, L., 1968, p.153
36 Saito, T., 1988, pp.10-15
37 Shigemori, M., 1965, pp.9-19
38 ibid., pp.19-57
39 Hennig, K., 1982, pp.204-223
40 Rajneesh, Bhagwan Shree, 1978, p.75
41 Hennig, K., 1982, p.284
42 Tanaka, I., 1972, p.60
43 Ibid., p.129
44 Nishiyama, K. and Stevens, J., 1975, p.91
45 Hennig, K., 1982, p.147
46 Itoh, T., 1977, p.239
47 Shigemori, M., 1965, pp.58-96
48 Hisamatsu, S., 1971, p.53
49 Kuitert, W., 1988, p.150, 159
50 Slawson, D., 1987, p.72
51 Ueda, M., 1967, p.65
52 idem
53 Bense, M., 1967, p.35
54 both quotations from: Komparu, K., 1983, p.73 f.
55 Slawson, D., 1987, Item 1, 2
56 ibid., Appendix 2
57 Hall, J.W., 1981, pp.7-71
58 Reischauer, E.O. and Fairbank, J.K., 1958, p.616
59 quoted from: Ueda, M., 1967, p.94
60 Shigemori, M. and K.: Taikei, vol.8, 1971, pp.3-12
61 ibid., p.19 f.
62 ibid., p.70 ff.
63 ibid., vol.9, 1972, p.42 f.
64 ibid., vol.10, 1975, pp.12-16
65 ibid., vol.9, 1972, p.16 ff.
66 ibid., p.53 ff.
67 ibid., vol.8, 1971, p.15
68 Ludwig, T.M., 1981, p.374
69 c.f. Hennemann, H.S.: Cha-no-yu, 1980, pp.30-39
70 quoted from: Furuta, Sh., 1964, p.94
71 quoted from: Ueda, M., 1967, p.88

72 Itoh, T., 1969, p.50
73 ibid., p.44
74 c.f. Tanaka, S., 1967, pp.94-188
75 Varley, P., 1973, p.202
76 c.f. Shigemori, M. and K.: Taikei, vol.16, 1974, p.92 ff.
77 ibid., vol.14, 1973, pp.84-92
78 c.f. Speidel, M., 1975
79 idem
80 Jinnai, H., 1987, pp.42-47
81 Nitschke, G. and Thiel, Ph., 1968
82 Varley, P., 1973, p.244 f.
83 Shigemori, M. and K.: Taikei, vol.27, 1971, p.12 f.
84 ibid., vol.28, 1972, p.6 ff.
85 ibid., p.16 ff.
86 ibid., vol.30, 1974, pp.117-123
87 Alhalel, 1989
88 Osho, 1990

Bibliography

Books and Essays in European Languages

Alhalel, R., *Conversations with Isamu Noguchi,* Kyoto: Kyoto Journal, No. 10, 1989

Ambasz, E., *The Formulation of a Design Discourse,* New Haven: Perspecta 12, The Yale Architectural Journal, 1969

Aston, W.G., *Nihongi-Chronicles of Japan from the Earliest Times to A.D.679,* London: G. Allen & Unwin Ltd., 1956

Bennet, Steven J., *Patterns of the Sky and Earth – A Chinese Science of Applied Cosmology,* in: *Chinese Science,* 1978, 3 : 1–26

Bense, M., *Semiotik – Allgemeine Theorie der Zeichen,* Baden-Baden: Agis 1967

Bohner, H., *Zeitenreihe der alten japanischen Gärten,* Hamburg: OAG Nachrichten, Dec. 1966

Eliade, M., *The Sacred and the Profane,* New York: Harper & Row, 1961

Fukuyama, T., *Heian Temples: Byodo-in and Chuson-ji,* New York, Tokyo: Weatherhill/Heibonsha, 1976

Furuta, Sh., *The Philosophy of the Chashitsu,* Tokyo: Japan Architect, June 1964 – Sept. 1964

Hall, J.W., *Japan's Sixteenth-Century Revolution,* in: Elison, C. and Smith B.L., *Warlords, Artists and Commoners,* Honolulu: University of Hawaii Press, 1981

Harada, Jiro, *Japanese Gardens,* Boston: Charles T. Branford Co., 1956

Hashimoto, F., *Architecture in Shoin Style – Japanese Feudal Residences,* Tokyo: Kodansha International and Shibundo, 1981

Hayakawa, M., *The Garden Art of Japan,* New York, Tokyo: Weatherhill, 1973

Hennemann, H.S., *Cha-no-yu: die Teekultur Japans,* in: Nachrichten der Gesellschaft für Natur und Völkerkunde Ostasiens, Vol. 127–128, Hamburg 1980

Hennig, K., *Der Karesansui-Garten als Ausdruck der Kultur der Muromachi-Zeit,* Hamburg: MOAG, Vol. 92, 1982

Hisamatsu, Sh., *Zen and the Fine Arts,* Tokyo, 1971

Horiguchi, S. and Kojiro, Y., *Tradition of Japanese Gardens,* Tokyo: Kokusai Bunka Shinkokai, 1962

Ienaga, S., *Painting in the Yamato Style,* Tokyo, New York: Weatherhill/Heibonsha, 1973

Inoue, M., *Space in Japanese Architecture,* New York, Tokyo: Weatherhill, 1985

Itoh, T., *The Gardens of Japan,* Tokyo: Kodansha International, 1984

—, *Space and Illusion in the Japanese Garden,* New York, Tokyo: Weatherhill/Tankosha, 1973

—, *The Development of Shoin-Style Architecture,* in: Hall, J.W. and Toyoda, T., *Japan in the Muromachi Age,* Berkeley: Univ. of California Press, 1977

Itoh, T., und Futagawa, Y., *The Elegant Japanese House – Traditional Sukiya Architecture,* New York, Tokyo: Weatherhill/Tankosha, 1969

Jinnai, H., *Ethnic Tokyo,* Tokyo: Process Architecture, No. 72, Jan. 1987

Kloetzli, R., *Buddhist Cosmology,* Dehli: Motilal Banarsidas, 1983

Komparu, K., *The Noh Theater – Principles and Perspectives,* New York, Tokyo, Kyoto: Weatherhill/Tankosha, 1983

Kuck, L., *The World of the Japanese Garden,* New York, Tokyo: Walker/Weatherhill, 1968

Kuitert, W., *Themes, Scenes, and Tastes in the History of Japanese Garden Art,* Amsterdam: J.C. Gieben, 1988

Ledderose, L., *The Earthly Paradise: Religious Elements in Chinese Landscape Art,* in: Murck, C., *Theories of the Arts in China,* Princeton, 1983

Ludwig, Th.M., *Before Rikyu – Religious and Aesthetic Influences in the Early History of the Tea Ceremony,* Tokyo: Monumenta Nipponica, Vol. XXXVI, No.4, Winter 1981

Morris. I., *The Pillow Book of Sei Shonagan,* London: Penguin Books, 1967

—, *The World of the Shining Prince,* Tokyo: Charles E. Tuttle, 1964

Nishi, K. and Hozumi, K., *What is Japanese Architecture?,* Tokyo, New York: Kodansha International, 1983

Nishiyama, K. and Stevens, J., tr., Dogen Zenji, *Shobogenzo, The Eye and Treasury of the True Law,* Vol.I, Sendai: Daihokkaikaku Publ. Co., 1975

Nitschke, G., *SHIME: Binding / Unbinding,* London: Architectural Design, No.12, 1974

—, *SHIME: Bauen, Binden und Besetzen,* Berlin: Daidalos 29, Sept. 1988

Nitschke, G. and Thiel. Ph., *Anatomie der gelebten Umwelt,* Zürich: Bauen und Wohnen, No. 9/10/12, 1968

Osho, *From the False to the Truth, Discourse 8, July 5, 1985,* India: Osho Times, 04/16/1990

Porkert, M., *The Theoretical Foundations of Chinese Medicine,* Cambridge: MIT Press, 1974

Rajneesh, Bh. Sh., *The Heart Sutra,* Poona, Rajneesh Foundation, 1978

Reischauer, E.O. and Fairbank, J.K., *East Asia – The Great Tradition.* Boston: Houghton Mifflin, 1958 and 1960

Seidensticker, E.G., tr., Murasaki Shikibu, *The Tale of Genji,* 2 Vols., Rutland, Vermont and Tokyo: Charles E. Tuttle, 1976

Shimoyama, Sh., *The Book of Garden,* Tokyo: Town & City Planners, 1976

Sierksma, F., *Tibet's Terrifying Deities,* Rutland, Vermont and Tokyo: Charles E. Tuttle, 1966

Slawson, David A., *Secret Teachings in the Art of Japanese Gardens,* Tokyo: Kodansha International, 1987

Speidel, M., *Japanese Places of Pilgrimage,* Tokyo: A + U, Nos.1 to 12, 1975

Tanaka, I., *Japanese Ink Painting: Shubun to Sesshu,* New York, Tokyo: Weatherhill/Heibonsha, 1972

Tange, K., *The Secret of the Rock,* in: »This is Japan«, Tokyo, c. 1962

Ueda, M., *Literary and Art Theories in Japan,* Cleveland, Ohio: The Press of Western Reserve, 1967, see Chapter 4: "Imitation, *Yugen,* and Sublimity – Zeami on the Art of the No Drama" and Chapter 6: "Life as Art – Rikyu on the Art of the Tea Ceremony"

Varley, Paul, H., *Japanese Culture,* Tokyo: Charles E. Tuttle, 1973

Varley, Paul, H. & Elison, G., *The Culture of Tea: From Its Origins to Sen no Rikyu,* in: Elison, G. and Smith, B.L., *Warlords, Artists and Commoners – Japan in the 16th century,* Honolulu: Univ. of Hawaii Press, 1981

Williams, C.A.S., *Outlines of Chinese Symbolism and Art Motifs,* Rutland, Vermont & Tokyo: Charles E. Tuttle, 1974

Glossary of Terms

Books and Essays in Japanese

Akisato, R., *Miyako meisho zue* (Illustrated Manual of Celebrated Places in the Capital), 1780

—, *Miyako rinsen meisho zue* (Illustrated Manual of Celebrated Gardens in the Capital), 1799

—, *Ishigumi sonou yaegaki den* (Transmission of Rock Compositions, Live Gardens and Eight Types of Fences), 2 Vols., 1827

—, *Tsukiyama teizoden,* Part 2 (Transmission of Constructing Mountains and Making Gardens), 1828

Horiguchi, S., *Rikyu no cha-shitsu* (Rikyu's Tea Houses), Tokyo: Iwanami Shoten, 1949

Kitamura, E., *Tsukiyama teizoden,* Part 1 (Transmission of Constructing Mountains and Making Gardens), 1735

Mori, O., *Heian jidai teien no kenkyu* (A Study of Heian Era Gardens), Kyoto: Kuwana Bunseido, 1945

—, *Kobori Enshu no sakuji* (The Work of Kobori Enshu), Monograph No.18 of the Nara National Institute of Cultural Properties, Nara: Yoshikawa Kobunkan, 1966

—, *Sakuteiki no sekai* (The World of Sakuteiki), Tokyo: Nihon Hoso Shuppan, 1986

Niwa, T., *Katsura-rikyu no tobi-ishi* (The Stepping Stones in Katsura Detached Palace), Tokyo, Shokoku-sha, 1955

Saito, K., *Zukai Sakuteiki* (The Classic of Garden-Making Illustrated), Tokyo: Gihodo, 1966

Saito, T., *Meien wo aruku: Muromachi Jidai* (The Japanese Gardens: Muromachi Period, Vol. 2), Tokyo: Mainichi Shimbunsha, 1988

Shigemori, M., *Nihon teien-shi zukan* (Illustrated History of the Japanese Garden), 24 Vols., Tokyo: Yukosha, 1936–39, abbreviated as "Zukan"

—, *Karesansui,* Kyoto: Kawara Shoten, 1965

—, *Teien no bi to kansho-ho* (The Beauty of Gardens and Ways to Appreciate it), Tokyo: Hobunkan, 1967

— and Shigemori K., *Nihon Teien-shi Taikei* (The Great Compendium of Japanese Garden History), 35 Vols., Tokyo: Shakai Shisosha, 1971–1976, abbreviated as "Taikei"

Tabata, M., *Kenroku-en – Seisonkaku,* in: Nihon no teien bi (The Beauty of the Japanese Garden), Vol. 8, Tokyo: Shuei-sha, 1989

Tamura, T., *Sakuteiki* (The Classic of Garden-Making), Tokyo: Sobo Shobo, 1964

Tanaka, S., *Teien-ron toshite no sakuteiki* (The Sakuteiki as a Treatise on Gardening), in: Geino-shi kenkyu, No. 15, Kyoto 1966

—, *Nihon no teien* (The Japanese Garden), Tokyo: Kashima Shuppankei, 1967

Tsukushi, N., *Amaterasu no tanjo* (The Birth of the Sun Deity), Tokyo: Kadogawa Shinsho, 1964

Yoshikawa, I., *Chozubachi: Teien-bi no zokei* (Stone Basins: The Making of Garden Beauty), Tokyo: Graphic-sha Publishing Co., 1989

cha-no-yu	the tea ceremony
chisen kaiyu teien	"pond-spring-garden for strolling" of the Muromachi era
chisen shuyu teien	"pond-spring-boating garden" of the Heian era
Daimyo	domain lords of the Edo era
dairi	residential quarters within the imperial palace
geomancy	Chinese natural science (Jap. chiso, "land physiognomy", or kaso, "house physiognomy") used to determine the most auspicious form and site of a house, city or tomb
ginshanada	"silver sand open sea"; surface of white sand raked in patterns of waves
go-gyo	concept from Chinese natural science describing the five evolutive phases of earth, wood, fire, metal and water
go-shintai	"abode of a deity"; may be an unusual rock, tree, mountain or even waterfall
gosho	"the august place"; today the name of the Imperial Palace in Kyoto
hako-zukuri	topiary technique of clipping trees into box shapes
hojo	abbot's quarters, surrounded by gardens on all four sides
hondo	main hall within a temple complex
Horai	symbol of the "Isles of the Blest"; may be represented as a mountain, island or rock. Motif taken from Taoist mythology, according to which there are five islands far east of the Chinese coast populated by immortals living in perfect harmony
ishi-doro	stone lantern
ishitateso	monks of the esoteric Shingon sect acting as semi-professional gardeners
iwakura, iwasaku	"rock seat", "rock boundary"; rocks venerated as divine
kaisho	building used by samurai for festivities
kare-sansui	small, "withered mountain-water" garden; as a dry landscape garden, the prototype of the Kamakura and Muromachi eras
kawaramono	"riverbank workers"; originally the outcasts of society, they gradually rose to the status of professional garden architects during the Muromachi era
Kojiki	one of the oldest Japanese chronicles, dating from 712
kyokusui no en	"Feast by the Winding Stream": a popular festival amongst the nobility

mandala	sacred diagram embodying originally Hindu principles of the cosmos
Manyoshu	"Collection of a Myriad Leaves": oldest anthology of Japanese poetry
Miyako meisho zue	"Illustrated Manual of Celebrated Places in the Capital" of 1780
niwa-shi	"garden masters": professional garden artists
o-karikomi	topiary art of clipping shrubs and trees into large shapes
Pure Land Buddhism	faith in Amida (Amitabha), a transhistorical Buddha of light and life who governs a Pure Land (Jodo) in the West; model of a paradise on earth
reihaiseki	a worshipping stone for ritual activities
roji	"path", "passageway"; designates the tea garden which leads to the tea arbour
Sakutei-ki	the oldest surviving manual of garden design, dating from the eleventh century
samurai	members of the warrior class
san-sui	"mountain and water"; Sino-Japanese term for landscape; one of the most important metaphysical concepts underlying garden art and painting
shakkei	"borrowed landscape"; technique of incorporating background scenery into the garden composition
shiki-e	paintings inside a palace illustrating the beauties of the four seasons
shiki no himorogi	sacred precinct strewn with pebbles in which ritual purification ceremonies are performed
shime	"bound artefact", indicating possession; the binding of grasses and trees was a mark of occupation or possession and hence of power
shime-nawa	the ropes delimiting a sacred area or sanctifying a holy object within a Shinto shrine
shinchi	"Ponds of the Gods"
shinden	divine rice fields; main hall
shinden-zukuri	palace and garden architecture of the Heian era
Shinto	"Isles of the Gods", also "Way of the Gods"
Shintoism	indigenous Japanese religion; as „nature Shinto" it stamped the Japanese formal language reflecting the fundamental values of ancient Japan: respect for territorial rights, worship of nature, sense of purity and rice cultivation
shishin-den	"the purple hall of the Emperor"; building at the centre of the imperial residential complex since Heian times

shogun	"commander-in-chief"; imperial generalissimo, member of the samurai class; supreme political leader during the Kamakura and Muromachi eras
shoin	the most sophisticated room within the residential quarters of samurai and Zen priests
shoin-zukuri	architectural style of the Kamakura and Muromachi eras
Shumi-sen	Buddhist mountain at the centre of the world, adopted from Hindu cosmology, in which it is also known as Mount Meru
so-an	"grass-thatched hut"; simple rustic tea arbour
Sukiya architecture	new style of architecture which developed out of the tea house in the Momoyama era
tatami	floor mat measuring 3 x 6 feet
tobi-ishi	stepping-stones
tsubo-niwa	garden in an inner courtyard
tsukubai	"place where one has to bend down"; rock group with water basin in which visitors to the tea garden wash themselves both physically and ritually
wabi-cha	simple tea ceremony; since the end of the sixteenth century Japan's most formalized style of tea ritual
Zen	from the Sankrit "dhyan", meaning "meditation"; Zen meditation is based on the belief that the sole path to enlightenment is ji-riki, "power over the self"

Prospect

The original title of this study – The Architecture of the Japanese Garden – was chosen to convey from the outset that a garden is architecture, that is, form designed and built by man.

An overview of human history through the millennia shows how architecture has slowly but surely infiltrated and penetrated almost to the heart of nature on this planet. But if there is any new trend in architecture worth mentioning and worth nurturing now, a decade after the writing of this book, it is surely the way that nature has taken her revenge and entered and penetrated architecture as never before, in conceptual discourse, in imagery and in actual design. In Japan a rooftop space on an office tower is now significantly referred to as a "Garden in the Air", and metaphors such as "Garden of Microchips" or "Electronics Garden" have sprung up as names for urban designs, while the theme of a recent competition for a new example of urban architecture was „Vertical Gardens". The urban revolution might very well be followed by a landscape revolution.

This awareness of the unity, interdependence and indeed inseparability of architecture and nature, which has taken mankind a long time to reach, is to my mind the only stimulus fertile and potent enough to bring about a new vision in architecture and a new concept – a sixth prototype – of the garden. The strong creative force at work here, not only in Japan but all over the world, is clearly "a sense of unity" or "a longing for wholeness". Buildings become landscapes. *Tadao* Ando's *Honpukuji* of 1992, the Water Temple on *Awajishima* Island marks the beginning of this integration of architectural and garden design. Now architecture and gardens have become inseparable. Within a new concrete space, completely new to our senses, we are confronted with an ancient lotus pond of mystic Indian origin.

The negative side of the recent honeymoon between the architectural and the garden designer is that it has forced the latter into the camp of the modern architect. Modern architecture is shaped not only by the needs of society, as one would expect, but also reflects the aspirations of a highly self-conscious and competitive class of professionals in their struggle for survival and self-expression. Form for the modern architect follows fashion rather than need.

The question is, why were gardens first created, and do we still create them for the same reasons? No animal makes a garden, although animals' nests and shelters are a form of primitive architecture. The garden could be said to stand at the crossroads of nature and culture, of matter and consciousness. It is neither purely the one nor the other; it discloses both in the form of human art. No doubt the making or mere contemplation of a garden fulfils a deep longing in us for a second, but now conscious re-union with nature, a longing to be whole again, even to be holy. Thus, a garden can, at any moment, provide a vital bridge between us and nature, and link us to our origin and to our future.